Joseph Stansbury, Jonathan Odell, Winthrop Sargent

The loyal verses of Joseph Stansbury and Doctor Jonathan Odell; relating to the American Revolution

Joseph Stansbury, Jonathan Odell, Winthrop Sargent

The loyal verses of Joseph Stansbury and Doctor Jonathan Odell; relating to the American Revolution

ISBN/EAN: 9783743355170

Manufactured in Europe, USA, Canada, Australia, Japa

Cover: Foto ©ninafisch / pixelio.de

Manufactured and distributed by brebook publishing software (www.brebook.com)

Joseph Stansbury, Jonathan Odell, Winthrop Sargent

The loyal verses of Joseph Stansbury and Doctor Jonathan Odell; relating to the American Revolution

# Munsell's

Historical Series.

No. VI.

THE

Loyal Verses

OF

JOSEPH STANSBURY

AND

Doctor JONATHAN ODELL;

RELATING TO THE

AMERICAN REVOLUTION.

———

NOW FIRST EDITED

By WINTHROP SARGENT.

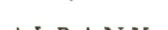

ALBANY:
J. MUNSELL, 78 STATE STREET.
1860.

Aux Lecteurs.

Amys lecteurs, qui ce liure lisez,
Despouillez vous de toute affection;
Et le lisant ne vous scandalisez.
Il ne contient mal ne infection.
Vray est qu'icy peu de perfection
Vous apprendrez ——   Rabelais.

growth of any school of fiction akin to those that had flourished on the other continent. The *Golden Legends* of the monks; the romances of knight-errantry; the satirical *Sirventes* of the troubadours—found no successors here. And while various circumstances hindered the new comers from bequeathing to this the local literatures of their own lands, other causes operated with equal force to prevent the early developement of anything like a national department of our own. Such tales and legends of those days as have come down to us are now as valuable for their rarity as for their nature. Obscure and remote, the Colonies for a long while scarcely claimed among themselves, and certainly did not obtain from Europe, the slightest consideration on the score of mental excellence or cultivation. So essentially were they in the shade, that it is told as a probable, if not a true story, that Cromwell would fain have sought refuge here, as in an impenetrable covert, from the wrath of the Court; and if his escape from the Thames was obstructed by the officers of Charles, it was in all likelihood because they conceived him about to fly into regions where it would be difficult to pursue and impossible to detect him. And many years later, when pious men from Virginia besought official favour in England to their scheme of establishing a College in that Colony, so slight was the esteem in which American intelligence was held that the Attorney-General

Preface.

General ſtared in utter amazement at the propoſition. "Why, what in Heaven's name," he exclaimed, "do "you want with a College in Virginia?" "To im- "prove the minds and the ſouls of the youth of the "province," was the humble reply. "Souls!" cried the law-dignitary, aghaſt at ſuch preſumption—"*Souls!* "*D— your ſouls! make tobacco!*"

Thus it happens that we find very little of local fiction in any of its ordinary forms, among our ancient American literature. The Revolutionary War, however, which gave this country a ſeat in the circle of empires, was ſucceeded by an unlooked for and wonderful proſperity, that ſoon raiſed it to greatneſs. And as this conteſt—the moſt important epoch in our national hiſtory—was not at all deficient in thoſe political verſes that naturally find their ſeat upon the lips of men engaged in a long and impaſſioned ſtrife, it does not ill become us, who today enjoy the fruit of the arduous toils of the founders of our State, to regard with an attentive eye every monument that remains of the characteriſtics of their nature. Nor ſhould the deſire to retrieve, ſo far as may be, every detail of the men and manners of that period, be dealt with as an idle inquiſitiveneſs, or ranked with that ſpirit which, as Sir Thomas Browne relates, would ſeek to know what ſong the Syrens ſang, or by what name Achilles was known among the women.

If

If then we cannot prefent the lays of minftrels, who

> In fage and folemn tunes have fung
> Of turneys and of trophies hung;
> Of forefts, and enchantments drear,
> Where more is meant than meets the ear;

we can at leaft effay towards recovering the party lyrics with which the contending ranks of our great civil war folaced their friends or provoked their foes: and if there be any truth in the propofition of Fletcher of Saltoun, that the fongs of a people control its action not lefs than its laws, the production would be juftified of every ftrain that can be fhown to have been born out of the popular troubles of that day. There is a clafs of ftudents who would gladly hear all that can be told of every thing which went to form the character and the habits of the actors in the memorable fcene: to whom no fact, however fmall, that relates to the grand event of the Revolution, is deftitute of intereft: and to whofe eyes the words of the *Old Turcum* fong, that cheered the American camp-fires in the fwamps of Carolina fourfcore years bygone, would be not lefs precious today than the prefence of the finger himfelf would have been to Tarleton while the Britifh ftandard yet waved in Charlefton; and thefe readers, at leaft, will not regard as altogether idle fuch collections as that here prefented.

Preface.

In gathering up the poetry of the Revolution, a peculiar intereſt naturally attaches itſelf to the productions of the vanquiſhed party. Of the ſayings and doings of our own ſide, we may be preſumed to poſſeſs at leaſt a certain degree of information: but of the Tory or Loyal party, the general reader can hardly ſay more than that it was numerous, brave, and intelligent; and that when it was ſwept away from the face of the land, its members ſeem to have vaniſhed from the public obſervation in the ſame moment with the cauſe which they had ſuſtained. Like Cardinal Beaufort in the play, it died, and made no ſign. The reader may, as he chooſes, continue with Warwick, that ſo bad a death argued a monſtrous life, or with the gentle king, lean to a milder judgment of the men who ſupported the cauſe of the crown. The queſtion is of no moment here; and it is of as little importance to determine whether their literary effuſions were poſſeſſed of any extraordinary merit. Their connection with the hiſtory of the times gives them value. The Engliſhman's boaſt, that he had ſung the laſt Stuart out of three kingdoms loſes none of its point becauſe the verſes themſelves have but little, and every modern reader would reſent the withdrawal from its appropriate place of the ſcurvy doggrel of *Lillibullero* as warmly as could have been done by My Uncle Toby himſelf, whoſe favorite reſource in time of trouble, was, it will be
recollected,

recollected, the whistling of that Williamite air. It is their political rather than their lyrical merit that has caused this collection of revolutionary verses: and although, in the Editor's opinion, they are wanting in neither the one qualification nor the other, yet it may be as well on the latter score to premise that the reader must not look to dealing with them simply according to their poetical desert. "Use every man "after his desert," says Hamlet, "and who should "'scape whipping? Use them after your own honour "and dignity: the less they deserve, the more merit "is in your bounty. Take them in."

But notwithstanding all that has been advanced, it may still be doubted whether it was worth while to disturb the repose of the pieces here printed. The Editor's interest in a favorite line of research perhaps disqualified him for an unbiassed decision: and an appeal to the judgments of friends was about as profitable as that of John Bunyan in a like strait;

> Some said, John, print it: others said, not so.
> Some said it may be good. Others said No.

Accordingly, as is not unusual in such contingencies, he has followed the counsel that agreed best with his own inclinations: satisfied that the limited impression of this book will at least prevent any very widespread dissatisfaction resulting from his proceedings.

In

In its preparation for the press, the Editor has been governed by the same rules that controlled the appearance of *The Loyalist Poetry of the Revolution*. The Notes are made purely with an intent to explain the author's meaning. To maintain or to impugn the sentiments expressed has been far from his plan. What incompleteness appears in the Notes is as much to be regretted by himself as by any other; their hasty preparation under circumstances that left him access to no other authorities than what his own shelves provided, may be suggested rather by way of explanation, than to justify any deficiency. In the selection of the matter for the text of this work, however, it has been thought well to join together the names and the remaining compositions of Doctor Odell and Mr. Stansbury, who were undoubtedly the two most important loyal versifiers of the time. A concurrence of fortunate circumstances gave the Editor access to what may be reasonably believed a complete collection of all that remains of their writings. Many of these were unpublished; many in the original manuscript; and narrowed as their list had already become under the hand of Time, there was every reason to suppose they would continue to suffer a yearly diminution. What estimate may have been placed on them by the opposing parties of the period in which they had birth, has not weighed at all to admit or exclude them from this collection; nor have

have the opinions their language conveys been regarded. When party heats run high, party judgments are of little worth. "Wit and fool," says Dryden, are consequents of Whig and Tory; and every man is a knave or an ass to the contrary side. This arrangement indeed falls more severely on the authors themselves than upon any others: for it cannot be denied that their productions, as here given, are of very unequal merit and comprise much that, in all probability, they themselves would on occasion have excluded. But the fault rests here with that Chance which, being no respecter of merit, has preserved indifferently a meagre assortment, in point of quantity, of the numerous writings of our poets, and in so doing has condemned their best and their worst efforts to a sort of Mezentian union: *Mortua jungebat corpora vivis.* All that remains for the Editor under these circumstances is to set in meet order and array the materials that he finds before him. Like Rob Roy, if they be 'ower bad for blessing, they are ower gude for banning:' and the most carelessly arranged line may perhaps be found to illustrate some neglected point of history.

Especial acknowledgments are due to Mrs. Charles Lee, of Frederickton, N. B., and to Mr. J. Francis Fisher and Mr. Charles M. Morris of Philadelphia, for their contributions to the text of this volume. The Editor would also remark here that from it he has
omitted

Preface. xvii

omitted two poems by Doctor Odell: *The American Times*, and *The Word of Congress*—which are already edited in *The Loyalist Poetry*. To the critical reader, who may object to the occasional omission of a phrase allowable enough in the last century, but too coarse for the more delicate palate of this, he would urge that in every such case a dash has been substituted for the discarded word; so, in the language of Peter Pindar,

—Let *thy* impudence supply the rhyme!

W. S.

Gloster Place, Mississippi,
    January 10th, 1860.

CONTENTS.

A Song,	1
On the Present Troubles,	3
When good Queen Elizabeth governed the Realm,	4
Inscription for Franklin's Stove,	5
Epigram,	6
Birthday Ode,	7
Song for a Fishing Party,	9
A Welcome to Howe,	10
A Birthday Song,	11
Tradesmen's Song,	13
The Fourth of July,	14
A New Song,	16
The Petition of Philadelphia to Sir William Howe,	17
Epigram,	19
The Kitten Song,	20
Verses to the Tories,	22
The Carpet Knight,	23
A Fable,	25

Table of Contents.

On the Downfall of Legal Paper Money,	29
Ode for the Year 1778,	31
A Pastoral Song,	33
A Song for the Times,	34
To Sir James Wallace,	35
The Church-and-King Club,	36
Church and King,	37
To Peace,	38
The Town Meeting,	39
The Congratulation,	45
The Feu de Joie,	51
Ode for the New Year,	58
The Lords of the Main,	61
Liberty,	63
Freedom,	64
On Admiral Arbuthnot,	66
A Pasquinade,	67
A Poetical Epistle,	69
Invitation,	71
Ode for the St. George's Society at New York,	74
A Song for St. George's Day, 1781,	76
On the Revival of the Church-and-King Club,	78
Song for a Venison Dinner,	79
The Royal Oak,	81
Woodlands,	83

Table of Contents.

A Christmas Song for 1782,	84
Let us be happy as long as we can,	86
God Save the King,	88
The United States,	89
Cordelia,	90
Notes,	93
Index,	189

THE
LOYAL VERSES
OF
STANSBURY AND ODELL.

THE
LOYAL VERSES
OF
STANSBURY AND ODELL.

A SONG,

SUNG AT THE SECOND ANNIVERSARY MEETING OF THE SONS OF ST. GEORGE IN NEW YORK, APRIL 23, 1771.

TUNE: *Black Sloven.*

[From Joseph Stansbury's Original MSS.[1]]

YE Sons of St. George, here assembled today,
So honest and hearty, so Chearful and Gay,
Come join in the Chorus, and loyally sing
In praise of your Patron, Your Country and King.

Tho' plac'd at a distance from Britain's bold Shore,
From thence either We or our Fathers came o'er:
And in Will, Word and Deed, We are Englishmen all;
Still true to her Cause and awake to her Call.

Let

Let Creſſy, Poiƈtiers, and let Agincourt ſhow
How our Anceſtors aƈted ſome Ages ago:
While Minden's red Field and Quebec ſhall proclaim
That their Sons are unchanged or in Nature or Name.

Should the proud Spaniſh Dons but appear on the Main,
The Iſland they pilfer'd, by Force to maintain,
The brave Sons of Thunder our Wrongs will redreſs,
And teach them again what they learn'd of Queen Beſs.

Tho' the proud Roman Eagle to Britain was borne,
Both Talons and Feathers got plaguily torn;
And Cæſar himſelf, both with Foot and with Horſe,
Was glad to ſneak off with—"It's well 'twas no worſe."

Tho' party Contentions awhile may run high,
When Danger advances they'll vaniſh and die;
While all with one Heart, Hand and Spirit unite,
Like Engliſhmen think and like Engliſhmen fight.

Then here's to our King, and Oh, Long may He reign—
The Lord of thoſe Men who are Lords of the Main!
While all the Contention among us ſhall be
To make Him as happy as We are made free.

And here's to the Daughters of Britain's Fair Iſle—
May Freedom and They ever crown with a Smile
The Sons of St. George, our good Knight ſo profound—
The Sons of St. George, even all the World round!

ON

ON THE PRESENT TROUBLES.

[Thefe Lines from the Stanfbury Manufcripts, have an interest as fhowing how fome even among thofe who, when War actually broke out, were unflinching in their Loyalty to the Crown, were at an earlier date difgufted with the minifterial plans for America. The author's confidence in the overwhelming Power of England is curioufly enough contrafted with his affertion of Colonial Innocence.[2]]

O N cryftal throne, uplifted high,
    Imperial Britain fate;
Her lofty forehead reach'd the fky;
    Her awful nod was fate:
Terrific Mars, with War's alarms
    Augments the pageant fhew;
And fea-green Neptune's circling arms
    Forbid th' invading foe.

Bright Science made her Name ador'd.
    Her robes the Arts empearl'd.
Wide in her Lap fair Commerce pour'd
    The Riches of the World.
Her Cheeks the Rofe in hafte forfook,
    By jealous Fears purfued:
Her Voice the Earth's firm Bafement fhook,
    And turn'd the Air to Blood.

Her Vengeance o'er the liquid Wave
    Explores thefe weftern Climes:
Juft Heav'n! a People deign to fave
    Whofe wrongs are all their Crimes!
        Cetera defunt.

WHEN GOOD QUEEN ELIZABETH GOVERNED THE REALM.

A Song.

TUNE: *Hearts of Oak.*

[From the Stanſbury Manuſcripts; and probably compoſed for a meeting of the Sons of St. George in 1774 or 1775.]

WHEN good Queen Elizabeth govern'd the Realm,
And Burleigh's ſage Counſels directed the Helm,
In vain Spain and France our Conqueſts oppoſ'd;
For Valour conducted what Wiſdom propoſ'd.
    Beef and Beer was their Food;
    Love and Truth arm'd their Band;
    Their Courage was ready—
    Steady, Boys, Steady—
To fight and to conquer by Sea and by Land.

But ſince Tea and Coffee, ſo much to our Grief,
Have taken the place of Strong Beer and Roaſt Beef,
Our Laurels have wither'd, our Trophies been torn;
And the Lions of England French triumphs adorn.
    Tea and ſlops are their food;
    They unnerve every Hand—
    Their Courage unſteady
    And not always ready—
They often are conquer'd by Sea and by Land.

St. George views with Tranſport our generous flame:
" My Sons, riſe to Glory, and rival my fame.
" Ancient Manners again in my Sons I behold

           And

"And this Age muſt eclipſe all the Ages of Gold."[3]
>> Beef and Beer are our food;
>> Love and Truth Arm our Band;
>> Our Courage is ſteady
>> And always is ready
> To fight and to conquer by Sea and by Land.

While thus we regale as our Fathers of old,
Our Manners as Simple, our Courage as bold,
May Vigour and Prudence our Freedom ſecure
Long as Rivers, or Ocean, or Stars ſhall endure.
>> Beef and Beer are our food;
>> Love and Truth arm our Band;
>> Our Courage is ſteady,
>> And always is ready
> To fight and to conquer by Sea and by Land.

INSCRIPTION

FOR A CURIOUS CHAMBER-STOVE, IN THE FORM OF AN URN, SO CONTRIVED AS TO MAKE THE FLAME DESCEND, INSTEAD OF RISE, FROM THE FIRE: INVENTED BY DOCTOR FRANKLIN.

[By Dr. JONATHAN ODELL.[4] 1776.]

LIKE a Newton ſublimely he ſoar'd
 To a Summit before unattained;
New regions of Science explor'd,
 And the Palm of Philoſophy gain'd.

With a Spark, that he caught from the Skies,
 He diſplay'd an unparallel'd wonder:
And we ſaw, with delight and ſurpriſe,
 That his Rod could protect us from thunder.

O had he been wife to purfue
    The track for his talents defign'd,
What a tribute of praife had been due
    To the teacher and friend of Mankind!

But to covet *political* fame
    Was, in him, a degrading ambition;
A Spark, that from *Lucifer* came,
    And kindled the blaze of *Sedition*.

Let Candor, then, write on his Urn—
    Here lies the renowned Inventor,
Whofe flame to the Skies ought to burn,
    But, inverted, defcends to the Center!

EPIGRAM

ON A SERMON PREACHED BY THE REV. MR. PIERCY, CHAPLAIN TO THE THIRD BATTALION OF PHILADELPHIA MILITIA.

[By JOSEPH STANSBURY. The late Rev. Dr. James Abercrombie, Rector of the united Parifhes of Chrift-church and St. Peter's, in Philadelphia (for notices of whom fee *Croker's Bofwell's Johnfon*, vol. III, p. 242, p. 285), who communicated this piece, could not fix its date, but believed it to have been written in June or July, 1776. "The weather being very warm," faid Dr. Abercrombie, "the fervant of General Roberdeau (who commanded the battalion), a very black and remarkably ugly Negro, ftood behind Mr. Percy, in the pulpit, fanning him with a degree of vehemence proportioned to his inflammatory addrefs."[5]]

TO preach up, friend Percy, at this critical feafon,
    Refiftance to Britain, is not very civil.
Yet what can we look for but Faction and Treafon
From a flaming Enthufiaft, fann'd by the Devil?

BIRTHDAY ODE.

[Written by Dr. ODELL, on occasion of the King's Birthday, June 4th, 1776; and sung by a number of British officers (captured at St. John's and Chambly by General Montgomery) who were prisoners at that time at Burlington, New Jersey; and who, to avoid offence, had an entertainment in honor of the day prepared on an island in the river Delaware, where they dined under a tree.[6] Printed from the author's copy, collated with a contemporaneous Manuscript.]

O'ER Britannia's happy Land,
    Rul'd by George's mild command,
On this bright, auspicious day
Loyal hearts their tribute pay.
    Ever sacred be to mirth
    The day that gave our Monarch birth!

There, the thundering Cannon's roar
Echoes round from shore to shore;
Royal Banners wave on high;
Drums and trumpets rend the sky.

There our Comrades clad in Arms,
Long enured to War's alarms,
Marshall'd all in bright array
Welcome this returning day.

There, the temples chime their bells;
And the pealing anthem swells;
And the gay, the grateful throng
Join the loud triumphant song!

Nor

Nor to Britain's Isle confin'd—
Many a distant Region join'd
Under George's happy sway
Joys to hail this welcome day.

O'er this Land among the rest,
Till of late supremely blest,
George, to sons of Britain dear,
Swell'd the song from year to year.

Here, we now lament to find
Sons of Britain, fierce and blind,
Drawn from loyal love astray,
Hail no more this welcome day.

When by foreign Foes dismay'd,
Thankless Sons, ye call'd for aid:
Then, *we* gladly fought and bled,
And your Foes in triumph led.

Now, by Fortune's blind command,
Captives in your hostile Land;
To this lonely spot we stray
Here unseen to hail this day!

Though by Fortune thus betray'd,
For a while we seek the shade,
Still our loyal hearts are free—
Still devoted, George, to thee!

Britain, Empress of the Main,
Fortune envies thee in vain:
Safe, while Ocean round thee flows,
Though the *world* were *all* thy Foes.

Long

of Stanſbury and Odell.

Long as Sun and Moon endure
Britain's Throne ſhall ſtand ſecure,
And great George's royal line
There in ſplendid honor ſhine.
  Ever ſacred be to Mirth
  The day that gave our Monarch birth!

SONG

FOR A FISHING PARTY NEAR BURLINGTON, ON THE
DELAWARE, IN 1776.

[Compoſed by Dr. ODELL, under circumſtances ſimilar to thoſe which occaſioned the preceding piece. To the third verſe he has appended this Note: "*Proteſtant* was a term adopted by a circle of Loyaliſts."]

HOW ſweet is the ſeaſon, the ſky how ſerene;
 On Delaware's banks how delightful the ſcene;
The Prince of the Rivers, his waves all aſleep,
In ſilence majeſtic glides on to the Deep.

Away from the noiſe of the Fife and the Drum,
And all the rude din of Bellona we come;
And a plentiful ſtore of good humor we bring
To ſeaſon our feaſt in the ſhade of Cold Spring.

A truce then to all whig and tory debate;
True lovers of Freedom, contention we hate:
For the Demon of diſcord in vain tries his art
To poſſeſs or inflame a true *Proteſtant* heart.

True Proteſtant friends to fair Liberty's cauſe,
To decorum, good order, religion and laws,
From avarice, jealouſy, perfidy, free;
We wiſh all the world were as happy as we.

We have wants, we confeſs, but are free from the care
Of thoſe that abound, yet have nothing to ſpare:
Serene as the ſky, as the river ſerene,
We are happy to want envy, malice and ſpleen.

While thouſands around us, miſled by a few,
The Phantoms of pride and ambition purſue,
With pity their fatal deluſion we ſee;
And wiſh all the world were as happy as we!

A WELCOME TO HOWE.

[Written by Joseph Stansbury, on occaſion of the arrival of Sir William Howe on the coaſt of New York, in June, 1776.]

HE comes, he comes, the Hero comes:
   Sound, ſound your Trumpets, beat your Drums:
From port to port let Cannon roar
Howe's welcome to this weſtern Shore!

Britannia's dauntleſs Sons appear;
For Ages paſt renown'd in War.
The Sword they draw, the Lance they wield,
Now Glory calls them to the Field.

With laurels crown'd triumphant ſee
Britannia's Genius, Victory:
With her, fair Freedom ſits in State,
And Mercy ſmiles, ſerenely great.

My

My Sons, Britannia cries—forbear:
Deluded Sons, nor urge the War.
What Juftice afks, is all your own;
For Juftice yet fupports my Throne.

Would you be free?—be Freedom thine:
Britannia bends at Freedom's fhrine.
Is Wealth your Wifh?—that Wealth poffefs,
For Britain's King delights to blefs.

Be happy ftill, nor dare explore
With moon-ftruck Guides the heights of Pow'r:
For Pow'r is mine, and flows from me
In temper'd Streams of Liberty.

With me connected, ftand fecure
While Sun or Moon or Stars endure:
And when the World is wrapt in Fire,
This mighty Empire laft expire.

A BIRTHDAY SONG.

[By Dr. ODELL: compofed at New York, in honour of the anniverfary of the King's birthday, June 4th, 1777; and printed in the Gentleman's Magazine for that year.]

TIME was when America hallow'd the morn
    On which the lov'd monarch of Britain was born,
Hallow'd the day, and joyfully chanted
        God fave the King!
Then flourifh'd the bleffings of freedom and peace,
And plenty flow'd in with a yearly increafe.
Proud of our lot we chanted merrily
        Glory and joy crown the King!

With envy beheld by the nations around,
We rapidly grew, nor was anything found
Able to check our growth while we chanted
        God fave the King!
O bleft beyond meafure, had honour and truth
Still nurf'd in our hearts what they planted in youth!
Loyalty ftill had chanted merrily
        Glory and joy crown the King!

But fee! how rebellion has lifted her head!
How honour and truth are with loyalty fled!
Few are there now who join us in chanting
        God fave the King!
And fee! how deluded the multitude fly
To arm in a caufe that is built on a lye!
Yet are we proud to chant thus merrily
        Glory and joy crown the King!

Though faction by falfehood awhile may prevail,
And loyalty fuffers a captive in jail,
Britain is rouz'd, rebellion is falling:
        God fave the King!
The captive fhall foon be releaf'd from his chain;
And conqueft reftore us to Britain again,
Ever to join in chanting merrily
        Glory and joy crown the King!

                      TRADESMEN'S

TRADESMEN'S SONG

FOR HIS MAJESTY'S BIRTH DAY, JUNE 4TH, 1777.

TUNE: *When Britain first at Heaven's command.*

[By JOSEPH STANSBURY, and first printed in the Pennsylvania Ledger, October 22d, 1777. The Ledger was a tory paper, issued weekly by James Humphreys, at Philadelphia, during Sir William Howe's occupation of that city. On the 4th of June the city was still occupied by the Whigs, and this song could not have obtained publicity before Howe's arrival without bringing trouble on its author's head.

AGAIN, my social Friends, we meet
To celebrate our annual Treat,
And with our loyal hearts display
This great, this glorious Natal Day:
    'Tis George's Natal Day we sing;
    Our firm, our steady Friend and King.

For Britain's Parliament and Laws
He waves his own Imperial Power;
For this (Old England's glorious Cause)
May Heaven on him its blessings shower;
    And Colonies, made happy, sing
    Great George, their real Friend and King.

Since Britain first at Heaven's command
Arose from out the Azure Main,
Did ever o'er this jarring Land
A Monarch with more firmness reign?
    Then to the Natal Day we'll sing
    Of George, our sacred Friend and King.

To Charlotte fair, our matchless Queen,
To all his blooming, heavenly line,
To all their Family and Friends
Let us in hearty chorus join:
    And George's Natal Day let's sing,
    Our gracious Father, Friend and King.[7]

And may the heavenly Powers combine,
While we with loyal hearts implore
That one of his most sacred Line
May rule these Realms till Time's no more:
    And we with chearful voices sing
    Great George our steady, natal King.

THE FOURTH OF JULY.

1777.

[R. CHUBB is the reputed author of these lines: but as they have also been attributed to STANSBURY, the editor with some hesitation gives them a place here. They are printed from the Pennsylvania Ledger of December 10th, 1777; collated with a manuscript copy. The text in the Ledger is prefaced by this Note: "The following was written in commemoration of the *glorious action* on the evening of the 4th of July last, when a party of *courageous Independents*, headed by some of their Rebel Chiefs, waged a most daring war against the unenlightened windows of the Quakers and other enemies to their ridiculous independent scheme in this city."[8]]

WHAT times are these?—a perfect riddle!
    Whence fled the scenes of former quiet?
Bless us—when Patriots strum the fiddle,
    And Generals form and head the riot!

The

The unarm'd Quakers and the Tories
　　Suſtained the honours of the night,
And ſtill their poor, unſhutter'd ſtories
　　Hang zig-zag trophies of their might.

See General Gates and Dicky Peters,[9]
　　With Jemmy Meaſe of noted worth;[10]
Richard and Tom the prime of eaters,
　　Like ancient heroes ſally forth.[11]

Our true Don Quixotes, by falſe gueſſings
　　Direct their calls and lead the van :
Miſtake the Tories for the Heſſians,
　　And Quaker for poor Engliſhman !

Illuſtrious Chieftains ! future ages
　　Shall mark your triumphs of the day.
While wide the patriotic Sages
　　Shall round the world your fame convey,

Still as a foil, ye new Law-makers,
　　To former happineſs remain.
Blunderers, go on : deſpiſe the Quakers—
　　You never ſhall their heighth attain.[12]

The wiſdom of their gentle ruling
　　Can bear the retroſpective view ;
And this, with all your boaſted ſchooling,
　　Is more than will be ſaid of you.

A

A NEW SONG.

TUNE: *Cæsar and Pompey were both of them*, &c.

[By Mr. STANSBURY: printed from the original Manuscript.[13]]

WHEN Britain determined to tax us at pleasure,
    We rose as one Man, and opposed the measure;
Not liking the Pilgrimage, I can assure ye,
Of going to England for Trial by Jury.[14]
    Therefore for Freedom alone we are fighting;
    For that sort of Freedom was not so inviting.

To Edicts of Britain subjection refusing,
We set up a Government of our own chusing.
The Guardians of Freedom resolv'd to maintain it,
And publish'd a long Bill of Rights to explain it.
    For its for Freedom alone we are fighting:
    The name of all names which true Freemen delight in.

We fondly imagin'd that all future Story
Should tell of our Justice, our Freedom and Glory:
We laugh'd at Oppression, not dreaming or fearing
That Men would be banish'd without charge or hearing:
    For Freedom indeed we supposed we were fighting;
    But this sort of Freedom's not very inviting.

If they with our Enemies have been partakers,
Then prove it in God's name, and punish the Quakers:
But if there is nothing alleged but Suspicion,
What honest Man's safe from this State-Inquisition?
    If such be the Freedom for which we are fighting,
    This sample, good Folks, is not very inviting.

When good Men are seiz'd on, who boldly defie all
The malice of Hell, and demand a fair Trial—
The cause of refusal you vainly dissemble:
"The Churchmen must bend, and the Quakers shall tremble."
   Since this is the Freedom for which we are fighting,
   The old-fashioned Freedom was much more inviting.

When Quakers and Churchmen have suffer'd your pleasure—
Their Worship and Consciences shap'd to your measure—
The Catholics then may expect Penal Laws,
Whereby we shall have one Religion and Cause.[15]
   This, this is the Freedom for which you are fighting:
   And let all who think it so, call it inviting.

THE PETITION OF PHILADELPHIA TO SIR WILLIAM HOWE.

[Written by Mr. STANSBURY, about October, 1777, and now printed from his revised manuscript copy, collated with the rough draft. The latter, by the way, supplies the names of *Price* and *Coffin* in the thirtieth line.[16]]

TO General Howe, Commissioner in chief
   To grant all injured Subjects *sure Relief*,
We, the Subscribers, beg leave to present
This State of Facts, by way of—*Compliment*:

That long before the date of Whig and Tory
The *Paper-Money* was this Country's Glory;
In all our Dealings did its Value hold
In fix'd *Proportion* to the Coins of Gold:—

That when the British Troops first took Possession
It pass'd as formerly by your Concession:—
That with the Fleet came up the *Merchant-Stranger*,
Who, by refusing, brought *it* into danger:
(Inform'd perhaps that still in Rebel's hands
Lay all the mortgage-Deeds and mortgag'd Lands,
And reas'ning thence have so mistook the Case
They hold the Money's tottering as *its base*)
And certain *Citizens*, we must confess it t'ye,
Have brought their Brethren into sad necessity.
  That if suppress, it may be mildly said
We have no *Medium* adequate to Trade;
And if the Army sell their Bills at all
Th' Exchange they sell at must be very small.
  That *it* received the *Sanction of the Crown*:
And many *Friends of Government* in Town,
Sold each *Half-Joe* for *Twelve Pounds*, Congress Trash,
Which purchas'd *Six Pounds* of this Legal Cash;
Whereby they have, if you will bar the bubble,
Instead of losing, *made their Money double*:
Then pity them, the widow and the orphan—
Nor heed the partial Tale from Price or Coffin.
  That in the Year (the famous) Fifty-Nine—
A Year which must in Britain's Annals shine—[17]
The Army *wanting Cash* obtain'd the Loan
Of Paper Money, Fifty Thousand Pounds:
By which their Bills, that scarce a Man would buy,
Advanc'd *Fourteen per Cent* immediately.
Its true the Army now has Cash enough;
And *therefore* should support our Paper Stuff.
  That a *large Sum*, collected with dispatch,
Lays in the Treas'rers hands to pay the *Watch*,
Who will *not take it*, unless in the Shops
And Market it will buy them Food and Slops.

Our

Our Patrole *therefore* will have *Guns and Swords*,
Inftead of Lanthorns, Staves, and empty Words.[18]
   That if you will affume our Load of *Ills*,
Our Paper's *ready* to exchange for *Bills*,
To pay our Friends in England with your *Gold*,
And leave your Officers our *Rags* to hold.
   Thefe and *more cogent* Reafons might be told
Why Paper Money fhould be par with Gold.

We pray the General in a general Way
Would grant Redrefs, and that without Delay,
And *Value* give the *Paper* we poffefs:—
And then—*We'll fign the long-fince penn'd Addrefs.*[19]

EPIGRAM.

["Wrote extempore by JOSEPH STANSBURY on feeing a thin, Sieve-like Blanket returned by General Howe, in lieu of a good *Rofe Swanfkin*, taken from a Quaker."[20]]

WHEN Congrefs had fled in a Fright from their Foes,
The Quakers they thought to fnug under the *Rofe*.
But *Billy*, who fees with the Glance of an Eye,
Soon found though the Quakers were grave, they were fly:
Refolv'd to diftinguifh the *good* from the *bad*,
I'll fift 'em, he cries, if there's fieves to be had!

THE KITTEN SONG.

TUNE: *Come my kitten, my kitten,* &c.

[Probably by Mr. STANSBURY: published in Towne's Pennsylvania Evening Post, December 2d, 1777, with this prefatory Note: "*Good Mr. Towne*—You must have heard of the association or agreement that the ladies of this city (Philadelphia) have entered into, in order to support the old paper currency which has received the sanction of our gracious sovereign; and of their determination to exert themselves, as far as ladies can, to restore it to its former value. Now you must know, Sir, I am a subscriber to that agreement, and being myself vastly fond of a little fun and harmless humour, have concluded, from your physiognomy, that you have no objection to either, I have therefore sent you a new song to an old tune. By inserting it in your next paper, you will oblige a number of ladies, and among the rest your constant reader, *Flirtilla*. Philad. Dec. 1, 1777." In many respects these lines will remind the reader of the childish nursery doggerel that supplies the air: but the circumstances under which they were composed constitute an interesting feature in the local history of the day.[21]]

COME all ye good people attend
    Pray hear what a new comer offers;
I've all sorts of good things to vend,
    If you will but open your coffers.
    Here we go up, up, up,
        And here we go down, down-e;
    Here we go backwards and forwards
        And here we go round, round, round-e!

Here

Here is a fleet from New York,
  And here the dry goods ſhall abound-e;
Here is both butter and pork,
  And all juſt now come round-e.

Here you have ſalt for your broth,
  And here you have ſugar and cheeſe-e;
Tea without taxes or oath,
  But down with your *gold*, if you pleaſe-e.

Here is an end to your rags,
  Your backs ſhall no more go bare-e:
Farewell to the ſneers of the wags,
  But your *gold*, Sir, muſt firſt take air-e.

Here you have good Iriſh beef,
  And here you have ſugar and ſpice-e;
Here you may part with your grief,
  For *gold* we have plumbs for mince pies-e.

Here you have topknot and *tête*
  Too big for a buſhel to hold-e;
Here you may dreſs like the great:
  And all for a trifle of gold-e.

Here you have catgut and gauze,
  And cambrick and lawn very fine-e;
Mits, hoſe, and a thouſand kickſhaws,
  For which let your *silver* be mine-e.

Here you have trinkets so fine,
  And baubles to hang by your ſide-e;
Here you may glitter and ſhine;
  For *gold* you may look like a bride-e.

Then

Then spurn at the wise old dons,
  Who make for their *paper* a rout-e;
Here's goods for your *gold* at once;
  Come, out with your *gold*, come out-e.

You'll ruin the land, we know,
  By joining with what we've told-e:
But since all your wealth must go,
  We'll strive to encircle your gold-e.

Come, surely I've told you enough!
  We have all that you want and wish-e;
But pray give us no paper stuff:
  We come for the loaf and the fish-e.
    Here we go up, up, up,
      And here we go down, down-e;
    Here we go backwards and forwards
      And here we go round, round, round-e!

VERSES TO THE TORIES.

[By Mr. STANSBURY. These lines appear to have been written in consideration of the hardships endured by persons who on the charge of being inimically disposed towards the interests of America, had been taken into custody by the Whigs, and confined in some interior and remote town.[22]]

COME, ye brave, by Fortune wounded
  More than by the vaunting Foe,
Chear your hearts, ne'er be confounded;
Trials all must undergo.
Tho' without or Rhyme or Reason
Hurried back thro' Wilds unknown,
                              Virtue's

Virtue's smiles can make a Prison
Far more charming than a Throne.
Think not, tho' wretched, poor, or naked,
Your breast alone the Load sustains:
Sympathizing Hearts partake it—
Britain's Monarch shares your Pains.
This Night of Pride and Folly over,
A dawn of Hope will soon appear.
In its light you shall discover
Your triumphant day is near.

THE CARPET KNIGHT.

[This piece, collated from two of Mr. Stansbury's Manuscripts, offers a renewed evidence of the disesteem into which Sir William Howe fell during his occupation of Philadelphia. The Tories were surprized and disgusted at seeing his fine army unemployed in any serious enterprise, and his splendid military capacities yielding to slothfulness, dissipation and extravagance; and, as many thought, even to avarice. The mortal whose charms were preferred, according to the song, to those of Venus herself, was probably a married lady from Jamaica Plains, near Boston, who is named in this same connection, but in rather broader phrase, by Francis Hopkinson, in his *Battle of the Kegs*. The date of this song seems to be December 24th, 1777; shortly after Howe's return to the city from his idle attempt to surprise Washington's Army at Whitemarsh.[23]]

LATE a Council of Gods from their heavenly abodes
    Were call'd on Olympus to meet;
Jove gave his commands from his throne in the clouds:
    Attend, and his words I'll repeat.

Ye

Ye know, all ye Pow'rs that attend my high Throne,
    Your Will to my Pleasure must bow:
I will, that those Gifts which you prize as your own,
    Shall now be bestow'd on my *Howe*.

Astræa, who long since had quitted the Earth,
    Presented her Balance and Sword;
The Honors derived from Titles and Birth
    By *Juno* were instant conferred;
Fierce *Mars* gave his Chariot; gay *Hermes* his Wand;
    Alcides, his Club and his Bow;
Sweet *Peace* with her Olive-branch graced his hand;
    And *Venus*, herself did bestow.

Thus, enrich'd with such Gifts as the Gods can impart,
    The Hero by *Jove* was address'd:
As you wish to reclaim each American heart,
    Let Justice preside in your breast;
Exhibit the blessings of Order and Peace
    As wide as your Conquests shall spread;
Let your Promise be sacred—Rebellion shall cease,
    And the Laurel shall bloom round your head.

I know that fell *Discord*, your zeal to oppose,
    Will nourish Sedition and Hate:
Mistakes may occur, and Friends suffer with Foes:
    Yet your Wish is confirmed by Fate.[24]
Sweet Peace shall revive from the horrors of War;
    Her Empire again be restor'd;
Affection and Duty shall cover each Scar,
    And *Howe* by the World be ador'd!

Now with shame must the Muse the sad sequel display;
    With Sorrow, and Shame, and Surprise:
The Gifts of *Astræa* he lost by the way,
    And her fillet he plac'd o'er his Eyes.

                                    The

The Arms of *Alcides* he fent to Burgoyne,
   And with them the Chariot of *Mars:*
For what but Affiftance and Weapons divine
   Could finifh fuch Quixotic Wars?

Hermes' Wand was now ufelefs; no Snakes would unite:
   The Olive in vain was difplay'd;
For bleffings no longer attended the fight,
   And Loyalty fled from its fhade.[25]
The Gifts fent to Burgoyne return'd to the fkies—
   Defpairing he yielded his Arms:
And fair *Venus*, difgufted, beheld with Surprize
   A Mortal preferr'd to her Charms.

A FABLE.

[Printed from Mr. *Stanfbury's* Manufcript, and bearing date January 24th, 1778.]

IN antient Times, the Poets fing,
   The Lion was elected King;
And all the Beafts, with homage due,
Proffer'd and fwore allegiance true
To him and to his heirs forever;
And fo far all went fmooth and clever.

But his dominions were fo large,
He could not execute his charge
And give his fubjects that protection
He promif'd them on his election,
Unlefs he call'd in fome affiftance:
For Brutes, as Men, will make refiftance
To lawful Kings, when at a diftance.

And, as he rul'd with feebleſt ſway
Where Pennyfeather's Foreſts lay,
He named the Leopard, Greyhound, Fox,
To hold them as with Bolts and Locks;
Three truſty Brutes to act together
As joint Viceroys o'er Pennyfeather.

Some time the project ſeemed to anſwer.
All day the happy Beaſts could dance, or
Sing and play a thouſand tricks;
Make bows or cringes; jump o'er ſticks;
And do what in their power lay
To pleaſe the Brutes who bore the Sway.
The Viceroys made ſuch large Profeſſions
Of guarding every Brute's poſſeſſions,
As private Virtue, public Zeal,
The good of all the Common Weal,
Alone inſpir'd their patriot Wiſh:—
No diſtant view of Loaf or Fiſh.
All ſelf and ſelfiſh aims ſubdued,
They lived but for the common good.

True Patriots are indeed a rarity;
And yet I may in truth declare it t'ye,
They dealt their Cards ſo well about
That no one entertain'd a doubt
But *Juſtice* had reſign'd her throne,
And left her Scales with them alone.

The tale proceeds: Upon the ground
An Oſtritch Egg one day was found,
By ſhipwreck caſt upon the ſhore.
The Beaſts the prize in triumph bore,
And laid it at their ruler's feet
With honour and obedience meet.

———— I must not dwell
Too long upon this precious shell.
What—but an Egg to be divided!
How can this business be decided!

Why, cries the Fox, this lucky Stroke
May be improved—the Egg's unbroke—
Then instant place it on the Strand,
And careful cover it with Sand;
Expose it to the Sun's warm beam,
And soon the Egg with Life will teem;
Produce a Bird of monstrous size
And weight and worth—a glorious Prize!
A Prize which we will share together,
Nor throw away a single Feather.

Sir Fox, cries Leopard, sure you joke,
Nor think how 'twill the Beasts provoke.
We rule with delegated Powers;
They think the Prize is theirs, not ours.
Oh, how our Cheeks will burn with Shame
When they traduce our public Fame,
And every Rascal cries at pleasure—" he
" Is one of those that robb'd the Treasury,
" And smuggled to himself the Gold
" For which the Egg should have been sold."
Let my advice this time prevail:
Expose the Egg to public Sale:
And whatsoe'er it shall produce,
Apply it to the public use.

The Greyhound paus'd—then thus began:
I much approve the Leopard's plan.
What he observes is very true;
The Rabble think the Egg their due,

And

And would with endless noise and clatter
Pursue us, if we smugg'd the matter.
What we *should* do is mighty plain:
What we may do, I'll just explain.
We may amuse the Beasts who crave it,
And say—the highest bid shall have it.
But few of them have seen such Fowl,
Or know an Ostrich from an owl.
Afraid the Bird may shortly die,
They'll cautious be, nor bid too high:
And those who know its worth and use,
Will swear they would prefer a Goose,
Or Hen that lays good store of Eggs:
That bating Feathers, Neck and Legs,
It was no larger than a Widgeon,
Nor half so fat as good Squab Pidgeon.
Then make a Bid with careless Air—
Not half its Value, you may swear.
Hence we may take a fair Occasion
And serve, each one, his own Relation,
In such a way, the candid must
And will acknowledge, strictly just.
Let's instant pay the highest price—
The Matter's settled in a trice—
And give our Friends the Egg to nurse;
The Public's serv'd—who fares the worse?
Pray, why may not our Puppies claim
Their honest share of Wealth or Fame,
And fill in time the higher classes?
And, cloathed with honor, be just Asses?

The Speech produc'd a general Smile:
And 'twas agreed to share the Spoil.

ON THE DOWNFALL OF LEGAL PAPER MONEY.

[Written at Philadelphia in the winter of 1777-8, by Mr. STANSBURY, and printed from a collation of his revifed manufcript copy with the rough draft. From the allufion in the fixteenth line, the piece would feem to have been addreffed to Rev. Dr. William Smith, whofe oration on the death of General Montgomery (Feb. 19th, 1776) was long confidered a model of patriotic eloquence. Literary taftes and a common religion may have eftablifhed a congeniality between Dr. Smith and the author which political prejudices need not have deftroyed.[26]]

WHEN Charles's Horfe, for want of Breath,
Like others fell a prey to Death,
No courtier dar'd to raife his head,
And tell the News, "that he was dead."
At laft they fix'd on Killigrew—
For what may not a Jefter do?
A licenf'd Wag, who, fpite of Rule,
Will fpeak bold Truths and play the Fool,
And tell a Monarch to his face
His Horfe is dead, if fuch the cafe.

In pride of War, when Heroes fall,
Then—Eloquence fhould grace the Pall;
In nervous Style their Worth proclaim;
And fix them on the rolls of Fame
In patriot ftrains, devoid of flummery,
Like your Oration on Montgomery.[27]

No Hero's praifes claim my Song;
No praife is due to acting wrong:

To burning, ſtripping, cheating, plundering:
Delays, Miſtakes and endleſs blundering:
Nor Charles's German horſe that's dead:
But faith, it is the *Want of Bread*,
Which threatens hard, (look e'er ſo funny)
Since the deceaſe of Paper Money.[28]

   Seiz'd by a Fit of Oppoſition
Which baffled ev'ry State Phyſician;
Each lenient Meaſure tried in vain
To bring her back to Health again;
Her nerves ſo firm and weak by ſpells;[29]
It poſed the Doctors Smith and Wells:
And when they order'd ſtronger Med'cines
She languiſh'd —puked—in fine, is dead ſince.

Ah!· what avails her former Pride,
When buſy Commerce roll'd his tide
Obedient to her nod? Her ſmile
Richly repaid the Lab'rers toil.
The regal Crown, with Splendor bright,
From her has aſk'd, and borrow'd Light.
Ah! what avails the Peaſant's cry:
The tatter'd Veſt: the aſking Eye:
The famiſh'd Look! the aking Heart:
The Infant's ſcream: the Parent's ſmart:
The fainting Wife: the Friend expiring,
For want of Food and Cloaths and Firing!

In this ſad Caſe, *Humanity* muſt fail,
Nor *Charity* can ſave the Wretch from Jail!
Both want the means to eaſe the victim's Woe,
Since *Gold* is Wealth, and *Paper* only Shew.
With heartfelt Sorrow then inſcribe her Urn,
And bid Poſterity the Story mourn.

INSCRIPTION.

INSCRIPTION.

Here rests, in hope some future Day to rise
With former Lustre in these western Skies,
A Heap of Paper, once by Britain made
The Life of Commerce, Agriculture, Trade;
The Sign of Wealth, and all that Wealth could grant;
The Friend of Man, the Antidote of Want!

Tho' by Rebellion now entomb'd awhile,
This seeming lifeless Heap again shall smile;
Again revive—exert her native Fire—
And shall with Britain flourish or expire!

ODE

FOR THE YEAR 1778.

[Printed from a contemporaneous Manuscript, and believed to have been written by Mr. STANSBURY.]

WHEN rival nations, great in arms,
    Great in power, in glory great,
Fill the world with loud alarms,
    And breathe a temporary hate:
The hostile storms but rage awhile,
    And the tir'd contest ends.
But ah! how hard to reconcile
    The foes who once were friends.

Each

Each hasty word, each look unkind,
   Each distant hint, that seems to mean
A something lurking in the mind
   That almost longs to lurk unseen;
Each shadow of a shade offends
Th' embittered foes who once were friends.

That Pow'r alone, who fram'd the Soul,
   And bade the springs of passion play,
Can all their jarring strings controul;
   And form, on discord, concord's sway.
'Tis He alone, whose breath of love
Did o'er the world of waters move—
     Whose touch the mountain bends—
Whose word from darkness call'd forth light;
Tis He alone can reunite
     The foes who once were friends.

To Him, O Britain! bow the knee.
His awful, his august decree,
    Ye rebel tribes adore!
Forgive at once and be forgiven:
Ope in each breast a little heaven;
    And discord is no more!

A PASTORAL SONG.

[By Mr. STANSBURY, and purporting to have been written at Mr. Smith's in the Summer of 1778.]

WHEN War with its bellowing Sound
    Pervades each once happy retreat,
And Friendship no longer is found
    With those who her praises repeat;
The good from the crowd may retire,
    And follow sweet Peace to the Grove
Where Virtue rekindles her fire,
    And raises an altar to Love.

There blest with a sociable few—
    The few that are just and sincere—
We bid the ambitious adieu,
    And drop them, in pity, a tear.
We grieve at the fury and rage
    Which burn in the breasts of our foes,
We fain would that fury assuage;
    We dare not that fury oppose.

With Peace and simplicity blest,
    No troubles our pleasures annoy:
We quaff the pure stream with a zest
    The temp'rate alone can enjoy.
Thus innocent, chearful and gay
    The swift-fleeting moments secure:
An age would seem short as a day
    With pleasures as simple and pure.

A SONG FOR THE TIMES.
1778.

[By Joseph Stansbury. This piece is a close paraphrase of *Plato's Advice* (Aikin on Song-writing, ed. 1810, p. 340), which itself was an alteration of the Rev. Matthew Pilkington's song, beginning, "Why, Lycidas, should man be vain?" The allusions are easily understood. In 1777, Congress had resolved that the stars and stripes should constitute our flag; and the treaty of alliance with France of February 6th, 1778, had inspired the Whigs of America with the utmost gratitude and confidence.]

SAYS Cato, why should Man be vain,
   Since bounteous Heav'n prescribes his dates?
Or seek with so much fruitless pain
   To form these independent States?
Can striped Flags with Stars bestrown,
   Or naked Wretches dragg'd to War,
Can upstart Honors e'er atone
   The pangs of Guilt or fierce Despair?

The Merchant's plan, the Farmer's toil,
   That rais'd our Wealth and Fame so high
And made our Plains like Britain's smile,
   In Dust without Distinction lie.
Go, search for Gold the public Chest,
   Where once abundance heap'd her store—
Our Wealth is Paper at the best;
   And all its Credit is no more.

What tho' the Frenchman crowns the scene,
   And we miscall him "Mankind's Friend;"
Not all his pow'r can Rebels screen—
   Rebellion's drawing near her end.

Shot like a Meteor thro' the Skies
It spread awhile a baleful Train:
But now, by Jove's command it dies
And melts to common Air again.

TO SIR JAMES WALLACE.

[These verses appear in Robertson's Royal Pennsylvania Gazette, March 24th, 1778; and are there credited to a New York newspaper. Their author is said to have been Dr. ODELL.[30]]

FYE! fye! Sir James! it cruel is
  Of the old Dutchman to make prize.
Tho', on enquiry, you may find
It was for good King Cong. designed,
Do'st think it is an honest job
This *Mity* bunch of Kings to rob?[31]
The Wine they want to cheer their spirits:
The Cordage to reward their merits:
Tea's now no more a cursed plant;
It now has Virtue—which they want.
Their Linen and their Silks return—
They're all in rags; their garments torn!
Yet e'en of rags nigh destitute—
The bullion which their friends recruit.
Tho' by *Experiment*[32] you find
Their Bark is Jesuits, rescind:
And I dare tell you, free as wink,
Detain their *Salt*, they then must stink:
Or, if you mean at all to save,
Their Brandy let the Varlets have.[33]

THE CHURCH-AND-KING CLUB.

[Written by STANSBURY, apparently in the latter part of 1778, for a feſtive meeting of a loyal aſſociation.[34]]

COME, honeſt Tories, a truce with your Politics;
   Hoc age tells you in Latin as much:
Drink and be merry and—*à Melancholy, nix!*
   'Tis de ſame ting do I ſpeaks it in Dutch.
If old Diogenes lov'd altercation,
   Had he, ſir, a drop of good Wine in his Tub?
Mirth and Good-humour is *our* occupation:
   Let this be the Rule of the Church-and-King Club.

Well do we know the *Adelphi's* miſcarriages,
   And the diſaſters of Johnny Burgoyne;
As to Beef-Stakes, no good fellow diſparages
   One who in *battle* finds *leiſure to dine*.[35]

Congo pretends (O good Lord, what a Fibber 'tis!)
   Now to *feel bold*, and to fear no miſchance.
As well might he ſay that he fights *for their liberties*,
   Whom he hath ſold in a *mortgage* to France![36]

Soon ſhall you ſee *a rebellious minority*
   Bluſh for the part they have acted ſo long;
Britain ſhall rouſe and regain her authority:
   Come then, a Bumper, and call t'other Song.
If old Diogenes lov'd altercation, &c.

CHURCH

CHURCH AND KING.

[Written by Joseph Stansbury *circa* January, 1779.]

IN days of yore when, free and unconfin'd,
   Man rov'd at large, and his own Will was law,
No ties restrain'd his selfish savage Mind;
The Mighty kept the Weak in slavish awe.
Till some sagacious Soul, pervading thro' the whole,
   To Harmony reduc'd each jarring string;
And now the tuneful Band obeys the Master's hand,
   While Echo sounds responsive Church and King!

In these, our vain and motley modern times,
When Whim, not Reason blindly leads the way;
And Virtue's varnish covers o'er our crimes,
Abhorrent to the honest face of Day;
Now Freedom strikes the Lyre, and vainly would inspire
   Celestial Ardor to each broken String:
But we despise the Foe, and by Experience know
   No Harmony's compleat without Church and King.

Tho' Rage vindictive Measures would inspire,
And hurl promiscuous Ruin far and wide;
Yet Mercy checks the British Hero's fire
And Pity gently pours her softening tide.
By Fate's supreme Decree this happy Year shall see
   The Royal Standard ev'ry Straggler bring,
Like Sheep, into the Fold from which they thoughtless stroll'd,
   To join in lasting Chorus of Church and King.

Then

Then, let each firm and trusty loyal Heart
Relate with glee his tale of suff'ring o'er;
And think with pride, he bravely play'd his part
And reach'd triumphant the long wish'd for shore.
The wreath let Victory twine, immortal and divine;
   The Laurel and the Bay let Fame now bring:
While Time shall hobble round, all Pleasures shall abound,
And the Virtues and Graces crown Church and King.

TO PEACE.

[From the Manuscripts of JOSEPH STANSBURY.]

O COME, light borne on eastern gales,
   And bid our sorrows cease:
With flow'rets crown our smiling Vales
Thou gentle Cherub Peace!
Efface the horrid marks of War;
Each private Grudge remove;
With Plenty load the rustic's Car,
And fill the Land with Love.

THE TOWN MEETING.

[This clever but bitter piece was written by Joseph Stansbury, and firſt publiſhed at New York in Rivington's Royal Gazette, No. 286; June 26th, 1779: under the title of *An Hiſtorical Ballad of the Proceedings at Philadelphia, 24th and 25th May, 1779, by a Loyaliſt who happened to paſs through the City at that Time, on his way from the Southward to New York.* It is here printed from the text in Rivington, collated with ſeveral contemporaneous manuſcript copies.[37]]

CANTO FIRST.

'TWAS on the twenty-fourth of May,
  A pleaſant, warm, ſun-ſhiny day,
    Militia folks paraded
With colours ſpread, with cannon too;
Such loud huzzas, ſuch martial ſhew;
    I thought the town invaded!

But when, on cloſer look, I ſpied
The *Speaker* march with gallant ſtride,
    I knew myſelf miſtaken:
For he, on Trenton's well-fought day,
To Burlington *miſtook* his way,
    And fairly ſav'd his bacon.[38]

With him a number more appear'd
Whoſe names their Corporals never heard—
    To muſter-rolls a ſtranger:
To ſave their fines they took the Gun;
Determined with the firſt to run
    On any glimpſe of danger.

The

The great *M'Clenachan* beſtrode
His prancing horſe, and fiercely rode:
    And faith, he had good reaſon!
For he was told that, to his ſorrow,
He, with a number more, tomorrow
    Should be confin'd in priſon.[39]

'Tis ſaid, ſome ſpeculating job
Of his had ſo inflam'd the mob
    That they were grown unruly;
And, ſwearing "by the Eternal God"
Such villains now ſhould feel the rod,
    Reſolv'd to "come on coolly."

The People's Majeſty—of Laws
The proper end, the only cauſe—
    Now ſhone in all its glory![40]
—*Morris* the wiſe; *Arnold* the brave;
The double *Maſon*; *Wiſtar* grave—
    Confounded with the Tory![41]

Nor age, nor wealth, nor rank, nor birth
Avail'd with theſe true ſons of earth,
    The offſpring of the Valley:
For all the lore of ages paſt
What car'd the Stateſman with his Laſt,[42]
    Or Hero of the Alley?

Cover'd with ſweat, with bawling hoarſe,
At cloſe of day no tired horſe
    More gladly reach'd his home.
Each doft his oaken civic crown:[43]
Firſt took a dram—then laid him down
    And dream'd of joys to come.

CANTO

CANTO SECOND.

Now Titan raiſ'd his flaming head,
And drowſy Centinels to bed
    Retir'd from irkſome duty:
For they were plac'd, as it behov'd,
To watch if Tory Goods were mov'd,
    That they might ſhare the booty.

The Mob tumultuous inſtant ſeize
With venom'd rage on whom they pleaſe;
    The People cannot err!
Can it be wrong, in Freedom's cauſe,
To tread down juſtice, order, laws,
    When all the mob concur?

But now, thro' *Mitchell's* brazen throat,
Faction with loud, abuſive note
    Proclaim'd a *Grand Town* Meeting:
Where printer's devils, barber's boys,[44]
Apprentice lads, expreſs their joys
    The Council Members greeting.

Each vagabond from whipping poſt,[45]
Or ſtranger ſtranded on the coaſt,[46]
    May here reform the State:
The Porter *Will*,[47] and *Shad-roe Jack*,[48]
And Pompey-like *McKean*, in black,[49]
    Decide a People's fate.

The Trained Bands of Germantown
With Clubs and Bayonets came down,
    And ſwell'd the motley train;
Reſolv'd to change, like him of old,
Old rags and lampblack[50] into Gold,
    Or Chaos bring again.

And now the State-houfe yard was full,
And Orators fo grave, fo dull,
    Appear'd upon the ftage:
But all was riot, noife, difgrace;
And Freedom's fons thro' all the place
    In bloody frays engage.

Sagacious *Matlack*[51] ftrove in vain
To pour his fenfe in Dutchmen's brain,
    With ev'ry art to pleafe:
Obferv'd "that as their Money fell.
" Like Lucifer, to loweft Hell,
    " Tho' fwift, yet by degrees —

" So fhould it rife, and goods fhould fall
" Month after month, and one and all
    " Would buy as cheap as ever;
" That they loft all, who grafp'd too much" —
(This Colonel *Bull*[52] explain'd in Dutch),
    — But fruitlefs each endeavour.

With folemn phiz and action flow,
Arofe the Chairman, *Roberdeau*,[53]
    And made this humane motion:
' That Tories, with their brats and wives,
Should fly, to fave their wretched lives,
    From Sodom into — Gofhen.'[54]

He central ftood, and all the ground
With people cover'd, him furround;
    And thence it came to pafs -
That, as he fpoke with zeal upon't,
He turn'd his face to thofe in front;
    To thofe behind, ———

                                  This

This gave offence—his voice was drown'd.
He should have shown his face all round,
    Like whirligig in socket:
Or, if that did his art surpass,
He should at least have ta'en ———
    And put it in his pocket.⁵⁵

Then *Hutchinson*,⁵⁶ that great bull-calf—
A gander has more brains by half—⁵⁷
    In croaking, froglike note
Approv'd the motion, and demands
The People's sense, by shew of hands,
    To save or damn the vote.

All rais'd their hands, with mighty burst
Of loud acclaim—The case revers'd,
    All lift their hands again!
Blue *Bayard* grinn'd—that long-ear'd ass—
With mobs he saw it was a farce
    To reason or explain.

But thoughtful *Rush*,⁵⁸ and artful *Gaff*,⁵⁹
And *Bryan*,⁶⁰ too much vex'd to laugh,
    Were fill'd with grief and pity;
And soon dismiss'd the Rabble Rout:
Concluding what they were about
    With chusing a Committee.

Hoping to get them more in tune
Before the twenty-fifth of June,
    Which was the chosen day
For them to meet by sound of Drum;
Unless the Enemy should come
    And make them run away.

To tell their Tale, away they fpeed
To their *prime mover, Jofeph Reed,*
    "*The virtuous and fublime!*"
So *virtuous*, that he cheats his friends,
Sublimely cheats to gain his ends;
    And glories in the crime.

Ambition is his darling theme:
Integrity an idle dream
    That vulgar minds may awe.
At home, abroad, with friend or wife,
In public or in private life,
    The tyrant's will is law.

Of deep refentments, wicked, bold,
The thirft of Blood, of Power, of Gold,
    Poffefs alternate fway:
And *Johnftone's* bribe had furely won
Rebellion's pale-fac'd matchlefs fon,
    Had *Mammon* rul'd that day.[61]

But time would fail me to rehearfe
In my poor limping doggrel verfe,
    His character divine:
Suffice it that in *Dunlap's* page,
Drawn by himfelf, from age to age
    It fhall with fplendor fhine![62]

THE CONGRATULATION.
A Poem.
Dii boni, boni quid porto.—TERENCE.

[Written by Rev. Dr. ODELL, on occasion of the failure of the great expectations entertained by the Americans from the presence in our waters of D'Estaing's fleet during the years 1778 and 1779. This piece appears to have been very popular at the period, being printed at New York in Rivington's Royal Gazette of November 6th, 1779; and again in the Supplement of November 24th.[63]]

JOY to great Congress, joy an hundred fold:
   The grand cajolers are themselves cajol'd!
In vain has [Franklin's] artifice been tried,
And Louis swell'd with treachery and pride:
Who reigns supreme in heav'n deception spurns,
And on the author's head the mischief turns.
What pains were taken to procure D'Estaing!
His fleet's dispers'd, and Congress may go hang.

Joy to great Congress, joy an hundred fold:
The grand cajolers are themselves cajol'd!
Heav'ns King sends forth the hurricane and strips
Of all their glory the perfidious ships.
His Ministers of Wrath the storm direct;
Nor can the Prince of Air his French protect.
Saint George, Saint David show'd themselves true hearts;
Saint Andrew and Saint Patrick topp'd their parts.
With right Eolian puffs the wind they blew;
Crack went the masts; the sails to shivers flew.
Such honest Saints shall never be forgot;
Saint Dennis, and Saint Tammany, go rot.[64]

                            Joy

Joy to great Congrefs, joy an hundred fold;
The grand cajolers are themfelves cajol'd!
Old Satan holds a council in mid-air;
Hear the black Dragon furious rage and fwear—
—Are thefe the triumphs of my Gallic friends?
How will you ward this blow, my trufty fiends?
What remedy for this unlucky job?
What art fhall raife the fpirits of the mob?
Fly fwift, ye fure fupporters of my realm,
Ere this ill-news the rebels overwhelm.
Invent, fay any thing to make them mad;
Tell them the King—No, Dev'ls are not fo bad;
The dogs of Congrefs at the King let loofe;
But ye, brave Dev'ls, avoid fuch mean abufe.

Joy to great Congrefs, joy an hundred fold:
The grand cajolers are themfelves cajol'd!
What thinks Sir Wafhington of this mifchance;
Blames he not thofe, who put their truft in France?
A broken reed comes pat into his mind:
Egypt and France by rufhes are defin'd,
Bafeft of Kingdoms underneath the fkies,
Kingdoms that could not profit their allies.
How could the tempeft play him fuch a prank?
Blank is his profpect, and his vifage blank:
Why from Weft-Point his armies has he brought?
Can nought be done?—fore fighs he at the thought.
Back to his mountains Wafhington may trot:
He take this city—yes, when Ice is hot.

Joy to great Congrefs, joy an hundred fold:
The grand cajolers are themfelves cajol'd!
Ah, poor militia of the Jerfey State,
Your hopes are bootlefs, you are come too late.
                                    Your

Your four hours plunder of New-York is fled,
And grievous hunger haunts you in its ſtead.
Sorrow and ſighing ſeize the Yankee race,
When the brave Briton looks them in the face:
The brawny Heſſian, the bold Refugee,
Appear in arms, and lo! the rebels flee;
Each in his bowels griping *ſpankue* feels;
Each drops his haverſack, and truſts his heels.
Scamp'ring and ſcouring o'er the fields they run,
And here you find a ſword, and there a gun.

Joy to great Congreſs, joy an hundred fold;
The grand cajolers are themſelves cajol'd!
The doleful tidings Philadelphia reach,
And Duffield[65] cries—The wicked make a breach!
Members of Congreſs in confuſion meet,
And with pale countenance each other greet.
—No comfort, brother?—Brother, none at all.
Fall'n is our tower; yea, broken down our wall.
Oh brother! things are at a dreadful paſs:
Brother, we ſinn'd in going to the Maſs.
The Lord, who taught our fingers how to fight,
For this denied to curb the tempeſt's might:
Our paper coin refuſ'd for flour we ſee,
And lawyers will not take it for a fee.

Joy to great Congreſs, joy an hundred fold:
The grand cajolers are themſelves cajol'd!
What cauſ'd the French from Parker's fleet to ſteal?
They wanted thirty thouſand caſks of meal.
Where are they now—can mortal man reply?
Who finds them out muſt have a Lynx's eye.
Some place them in the ports of Cheſapeak;
Others account them bound to Martinique;

Some

Some think to Bofton they intend to go;
And fome fuppofe them in the deep below.
One thing is certain, be they where they will,
They keep their triumph moft exceeding ftill.
They have not even Pantagruel's luck,
Who conquer'd two old women and a duck.⁶⁶

Joy to great Congrefs, joy an hundred fold:
The grand cajolers are themfelves cajol'd!
How long fhall the deluded people look
For the French fquadron moor'd at Sandy Hook?
Of all their hopes the comfort and the ftay,
This vile deceit at length muft pafs away.
What impofition can be thought on next,
To cheer their partizans, with doubt perplex'd?
Dollars on dollars heap'd up to the fkies,
Their value finks the more, the more they rife;
Bank notes of bankrupts, ftruck without a fund,
Puff'd for a feafon, will at laft be fhunn'd.
Call forth invention, ye renown'd in guile;
New falfehoods frame in matter, and in ftyle;
Send fome enormous fiction to the prefs;
Again prepare the circular addrefs;
With lies, with nonfenfe, keep the people drunk:
For fhould they once reflect, your power is funk.

Joy to great Congrefs, joy an hundred fold:
The grand cajolers are themfelves cajol'd!
The farce of empire will be finifh'd foon,
And each mock-monarch dwindle to a loon.
Mock-money and mock-ftates fhall melt away,
And the mock-troops difband for want of pay.
Ev'n now decifive ruin is prepar'd:
Ev'n now the heart of Huntington is fcar'd.⁶⁷

Seen

Seen or unseen, on earth, above, below,
All things conspire to give the final blow.
Heaven has ten thousand thunderbolts to dart;
From Hell, ten thousand livid flames will start;
Myriads of swords are ready for the field;
Myriads of lurking daggers are conceal'd;
In injur'd bosoms dark revenge is nurst:
Yet but a moment, and the storm shall burst.

Joy to great Congress, joy an hundred fold:
The grand cajolers are themselves cajol'd!
Now War, suspended by the scorching heat,
Springs from his tent, and shines in arms complete.
Now Sickness, that of late made heroes pale,
Flies from the keenness of the northern gale.
Firmness and Enterprize, united, wait
The last command, to strike the stroke of Fate.
Now Boston trembles; Philadelphia quakes;
And Carolina to the center shakes.
There is, whose councils the just moment scan:
Whose wisdom meditates the mighty plan:
He, when the season is mature, shall speak;
All Heaven shall plaud him, and all Hell shall shriek.
At his dread fiat tumult shall retire;
Abhorr'd rebellion sicken and expire;
The fall of Congress prove the world's relief;
And deathless glory crown the god-like Chief!

Joy to great Congress, joy an hundred fold:
The grand cajolers are themselves cajol'd!
What now is left of Continental brags?
Taxes unpaid, tho' payable in rags.
What now remains of Continental force?
Battalions mould'ring: Waste without resource.

What rests there yet of Continental Sway?
A ruin'd People, ripe to disobey.
Hate now of men, and soon to be the Jest;
Such is your fate, ye Monsters of the West!
Yet must on every face a smile be worn,
While every breast with agony is torn.
Hopeless yourselves, yet hope you must impart,
And comfort others with an aching heart.
Ill-fated they who, lost at home, must boast
Of help expected from a foreign coast:
How wretched is their lot, to France and Spain
Who look for succour, but who look in vain.

Joy to great Congress, joy an hundred fold:
The grand cajolers are themselves cajol'd!
Courage, my boys; dismiss your chilling fears:
Attend to me, I'll put you in your geers.
Come, I'll instruct you how to advertize
Your missing friends, your hide-and-seek Allies.
O YES!—If any man alive will bring
News of the squadron of the Christian King:
If any man will find out Count D'Estaing,
With whose scrub actions both the Indies rang:
If any man will ascertain on oath
What has become of Monsieur de la Mothe:[68]
Whoever these important points explains,
Congress will nobly pay him for his pains,
Of pewter dollars, what both hands can hold,
A thimble-full of plate, a mite of gold;
The lands of some big Tory he shall get,
And start a famous Colonel *en brevet:*
And last to honour him (we scorn to bribe)
We'll make him chief of the *Oneida* Tribe![69]

THE

THE FEU DE JOIE.

A Poem.

Urgetur pugna Congressus iniqua.—VIRGIL.

[Written by the Rev. Dr. ODELL, and printed here from Rivington's Royal Gazette of November 24th, 1779. The gallant and successful defence of Savannah by the British under Prevost, Maitland, and Moncrieffe, and the final repulse of the Allies led by Lincoln and D'Estaing, on the 9th of October, 1779, occasioned great exultation in the British army at New York, and gave origin to these verses. Their title relates to the custom of celebrating any victory or other occasion of triumph in the American (and perhaps in the British) Army, by a general discharge of firearms.]

LET songs of triumph every voice employ,
   And every Muse discharge a *feu de joie!*
Hail, Congress, hail! magnificent, renown'd:
Rejoice, be merry; the lost Sheep is found!
You, Congress, knew him by his graceful bleat.
We only know him by his foul defeat.
Great Bell Wether, he led his scabby flock
In apt conjunction with the rebel stock.
He came, he push'd, he fled with half his train;
While sav'd Savannah swell'd with heaps of slain.

Let songs of triumph every voice employ,
   And every Muse discharge a feu de joie!
What awful silence thro' the land prevail'd
Since Count D'Estaing from St. Domingo sail'd.
No voice, no breath, no sound, no rumour flew,
Lest Parker should with all his fleet pursue.[70]

No whisper; no report—but all was mum,
Left reinforcements from New York should come.
To catch the British napping was their thought:
Now, by my faith, a Tartar have they caught.

Let songs of triumph every voice employ,
And every Muse discharge a feu de joie!
The French, entangled in a dreadful scrape,
From the West-Indies made a fine escape.
Arriv'd upon the coast, the scene was chang'd:
Uncivil Winds their armament derang'd;
Their first reception was exceeding rough;
Howe'er they landed: landed sure enough.
Ashore, they vapour and defy the Storm,
And soon with *Lincoln's* troops a junction form.

Let songs of triumph every voice employ,
And every Muse discharge a feu de joie!
Plunder's the Word; but Plunder soon is o'er.
Rob folks of all, and you can rob no more.
Live stock or dead, they capture and condemn:
Come Whig, come Tory, 'tis the same to them.
The Continental gentry stand aghast
To see their good Allies devour so fast.
Are these the Troops of Louis, Friend of Men?
They're rather Tygers, loosen'd from a Den.

Let songs of triumph every voice employ,
And every Muse discharge a feu de joie!
The sworn confederates manfully advance
In quest of Glory and the Good of France.
Go summon, Trumpeter, yon haughty Town:
Bid them surrender to the Gallic Crown.[71]
What, are they restiff?—scorn they to obey?
Peste—we'll compel them with what speed we may.

            Erect

Erect your batteries, Engineers, in haste:
Mortars and Cannons in the Works be plac'd.
Upon the right my valiant French shall load;
You Continentals, line th' Augusta road.
Moncrieffe seems active, but he'll soon be sick,
When shells and balls and bullets rattle thick.[72]

Let songs of triumph every voice employ,
And every Muse discharge a feu de joie!
The brave D'Estaing encourages his troops,
And promises good store of drams and soups.
Work on, work on, ye jolly Pioneers.
The town shall soon be knock'd about their ears.
Meantime, strict guard about the camp we'll keep,
And neither in nor out a mouse shall creep.
But whence arises, in the dead of night,
This horrid noise to fill us with affright?
Are all the devils got loose?—D'Estaing cries out.
—No, sir, 'tis Maitland puts us to the rout.[73]
Stop him this instant!—Sir, he won't be stopt.
Chop him—*En verite*, ourselves are chopt.
The town he shall not enter, I declare,
—True, noble Count, for he's already there.

Let songs of triumph every voice employ,
And every Muse discharge a feu de joie!
The Gallic Chief, his batteries complete,
Conceives the British humbled at his feet.
Full thirty cannons, mortars half a score;
No doubt Prevost must tremble at their roar.
They open, and proclaim Savannah's doom;
Hide day with smoke, with flashes night illume.
Now whistle through the air the pond'rous plumbs;
Now mount aloft, and now descend the bombs.
Incessant thunders rend the frighted sky,
And bluffs and hillocks to the sound reply.

Let songs of triumph every voice employ,
And every Muse discharge a feu de joie!
What great effect has all this fire produc'd?
Here falls an house, and there a turf is loos'd.
What, no slain warriors tumbled in the trench?
Yes, by the Mass:—abundance of the French!
No cannon yet dismounted can you see?
Oh yes—a number marked with *Fleurs de Lys*.
Where are the Yankees?—where they were at first.
What have we got then?—we have got the worst.
How can this be? Six days, and nothing done!
The case is plain—the foe gives three for one.
Our thirty cannon have no chance at all,
Moncrieffe salutes with ninety from the wall.
Pize on't—this way of siege is most absurd:
We'll have no more on't—Storm shall be the word!

Let songs of triumph every voice employ,
And every Muse discharge a feu de joie!
The Veterans of France have form'd the line,
Expecting daybreak and the promis'd sign.
The Rebel Bands are marshall'd in array,
Boastful and loud, and covetous of prey.
What held the Town of beauty, wealth, and power,
Was all devoted in that cruel hour.
Sore sigh'd the Mother, for her Babes afraid;
And, anxious for herself, the blooming Maid.
The Merchant trembled for his crouded store:
One dreadful pause—and all perhaps is gore!
So to the rock Andromeda lay bound,
When rose the Monster from the vast profound:
But soon her brave Deliverer fac'd the foe;
No matter whether *Perseus* or *Prevost*.
His winged courser gallant he bestrode;
He look'd a Hero, and he mov'd a God!

He

He met the Monster in his fierce attack,
And to old Ocean headlong drove him back.

Let songs of triumph every voice employ,
And every Muse discharge a feu de joie!
Lo! from the Artillery pours the grand salute:
Then Silence flows—and all is hush'd and mute.
Sudden the drum rebellows; swells the fife;
And all move forward to the mortal strife.
The shouting warriors and the trumpets shrill
The meanest heart with martial ardour fill.
With rapid march advance the hostile rows,
While British fire the ranks tremendous mows.
Now nearer still and nearer they engage,
And War puts on accumulated rage.
There is the din of battle; there the crash;
The roaring volley, and the frequent flash.
There animation in the front appears:
There charge the chosen Gallic Grenadiers.
There, where each moment death they take or give,
Scarce Immortality herself could live!

Let songs of triumph every voice employ,
And every Muse discharge a feu de joie!
Now Slaughter triumphed and resistless strow'd
With mangled carcasses the reeking road.
Ev'n then, when blood was streaming like a fount,
Polaski rush'd the strong Redoubt to mount.
Again the grape-shot thunders from the walls:
He falls—half hero, half a fiend, he falls.
Off from the field his soldiers bear their chief;
Art was invok'd, but Art gave no relief;
Deep in his groin was fix'd the deadly wound.
Worthless, tho' brave, a glorious fate he found.

Such noble death what right had he to hope,
Whofe odius Treafon merited a Rope?
Undaunted minds were made in verfe to fhine?
But hate to parricides blots out the line.
Not Valour's felf the Traitor can excufe:
Him Truth condemns: him execrates the Mufe.[74]

Let fongs of triumph every voice employ,
And every Mufe difcharge a feu de joie!
Such defperate efforts the battalions thin.
Diforder and difmay and rout begin.
The worn brigades from fight recoiling fwerve;
Their courage droops, they faint in every nerve.
Yet ftill remains an excellent refource—
Bring to the charge the Continental Force.
What ails thefe Braggadocios of the Land?
Won't they come forward?—ftiff as Pofts they ftand.
Strange petrifaction on their hoft attends.
Deuce take the fools, they level at their friends!
Some angry Demon fure their fenfe mifleads;
See, the French tremble, and their General bleeds.
By rebel hands (Lo! Providence is juft)
The rebels' patron wounded bites the duft.[75]

Let fongs of triumph every voice employ,
And every Mufe difcharge a feu de joie!
'Tis done: Confufion fits on every face;
Inevitable ruin; foul difgrace.
Now Terror domineers, and wild Affright:
No hope in Arms: no fafety but in Flight.
Now, Britons, Heffians and Provincials pour:
Arreft the fugitives and bathe in gore.
'Tis done:—D'Eftaing betakes him to his fhip;
To Charleftown Yankies thro' the forefts flip.

Go

Go reckon up thy loss, amphibious Count;
Mark Fifteen Hundred to the full amount:
Of wounded and of killed an equal train
Left Lincoln weltering on the bloody plain:
Whilst forty Britons on the list appear.
O Earth confess, the Hand of Heaven was here!

Let songs of triumph every voice employ,
And every Muse discharge a feu de joie!
Does Lordly Congress relish this defeat—
Say, is it pleasant to their souls and sweet?
What, both o'erthrown, America and France,
By one small splinter of the British Lance!
Yet these were they, gigantic in their boast,
Who swore to chase us from this Western Coast:
Yet these were they who built flat-bottomed boats,
And vow'd to drive us like a Flock of Goats.
Unstable as the sand, their arts shall fail:
As water weak, they never shall prevail.
These, Reuben-like, their parent's couch defile;
Like Judas, these shall perish in their guile.
Could the Sword spare them, yet of Heaven accurst
Their very Bowels would asunder burst.

Let songs of triumph every voice employ,
And every Muse discharge a feu de joie!
Ye poor deluded owners of the soil,
For others' good who labour and who toil—
Ye wretches doom'd to sorrowful mistake,
Who hunger and who thirst for Congress' sake—
Arouse for Shame: like Men your rights resume,
And send your Tyrants to the Land of Gloom.
If Shame prevail not, still let Wisdom plead.
If both are slighted, Vengeance must succeed.

Your Parent State grows ſtronger every hour;
As yet, its Mercy far exceeds its Power.
Your Congreſs every moment weaker grows.
Rags are its Treaſure: Honeſt Men its Foes.
Its Building cracks, tho' buttreſs'd by the Gaul:
It nods, it ſhakes, it totters to its fall.
O ſave yourſelves before it is too late!
O ſave your Country from impending Fate!
Leave thoſe, whom Juſtice muſt at length deſtroy.
Repent, come over, and partake our joy.

ODE FOR THE NEW YEAR.

[Written at New York, January 1ſt, 1780, by Dr. ODELL, and now printed from his Manuſcript copy.]

WHEN rival Nations firſt deſcried,
    Emerging from the boundleſs Main
This Land by Tyrants yet untried,
On high was ſung this lofty ſtrain:
Riſe Britannia beaming far!
Riſe bright Freedom's morning ſtar!

To diſtant Regions unexplor'd
Extend the bleſſings of thy ſway;
To yon benighted World afford
The light of thy all-chearing ray;
Riſe Britannia, riſe bright ſtar!
Spread thy radiance wide and far!

The shoots of Science rich and fair,
Transplanted from thy fostering Isle
And by thy Genius nurtur'd there,
Shall teach the Wilderness to smile.
Shine, Britannia, rise and shine!
To bless Mankind the task be thine!

Nor shall the Muses now disdain
To find a new Asylum there:
And ripe for harvest see the plain,
Where lately rov'd the prowling Bear.
Plume, Britannia, plume thy wing!
Teach the savage Wild to sing!

From thee descended, there the Swain
Shall arm the Port and spread the Sail,
And speed his traffick o'er the Main
With skill to brave the sweeping Gale;
Skill, Britannia, taught by thee,
Unrivall'd Empress of the Sea!

This high and holy strain how true
Had now from age to age been shown;
And to the World's admiring view
Rose Freedom's transatlantic throne:
Here, Britannia, here thy fame
Long did we with joy proclaim.

But ah! what frenzy breaks a band
Of love and union held so dear!
Rebellion madly shakes the land,
And love is turn'd to hate and fear.
Here, Britannia, here at last
We feel Contagion's deadly blast.

Thus

Thus blind, alas ! when all is well,
Thus blind are Mortals here below:
As when apoftate Angels fell,
Ambition turns our blifs to woe.
Now, Britannia, now beware:
For other conflicts now prepare !

By thee controul'd for ages paft,
See now half Europe in array :
For wild Ambition hopes at laft
To fix her long projected fway.
Rife, Britannia, rife again
The fcourge of haughty France and Spain !

The howling tempeft fiercely blows,
And Ocean rages in the ftorm :
'Tis then the fearlefs Pilot fhows
What Britifh courage can perform.
Rule, Britannia, rule the waves
And ruin all intruding flaves !

THE LORDS OF THE MAIN.

TUNE: *Nottingham Ale.*

[Publiſhed at New York, February 16th, 1780, in Rivington's Royal Gazette, and believed to have been written by STANSBURY. In this, as in the piece immediately preceding, reference is made to the hoſtilities between Spain and England which had broken out in the paſt ſummer. The other alluſions to Carpenter's Hall at Philadelphia, where Congreſs met; to Congreſs itſelf, and to the French Alliance, will be readily underſtood. The tenth line of the laſt Stanza ſeems to have been a favorite: it is already uſed by the poet in an earlier page of this volume.]

WHEN Faction, in league with the treacherous Gaul,
 Began to look big and paraded in ſtate;
A meeting was held at *Credulity Hall,*
 And Echo proclaim'd their Ally *good and great!*
  By ſea and by land
  Such wonders are plann'd;
No leſs than the bold Britiſh Lion to chain!
  Well hove! ſays *Jack Lanyard,*
  French, Congo and Spaniard,
Have at you—remember we're Lords of the Main!
 Lords of the Main—aye, Lords of the Main;
The Tars of Old England are Lords of the Main.

Though party-contention a while may perplex,
 And lenity hold us in doubtful ſuſpenſe;
If perfidy rouſe, or ingratitude vex
 In defiance of Hell we'll chaſtiſe the offence.
  When danger alarms,
  'Tis then that in arms
        United

United we rush on the foe with disdain:
    And when the storm rages
    It only presages
Fresh triumphs to Britons, as Lords of the Main.
  Lords of the Main—ay, Lords of the Main—
Let *Thunder* proclaim it, we're Lords of the Main.

Then Britons, *strike home*—make sure of your blow:
  The chase is in view; never mind a lee-shore.
With vengeance o'ertake the confederate foe:
  'Tis now we may rival our heroes of yore!
    Brave *Anson* and *Drake*,
    Hawke, *Russell* and *Blake*,
With ardour like your's we defy France and Spain!
    Combining with *Treason*
    They're deaf to all reason:
Once more let them *feel* we are Lords of the Main.
  Lords of the Main—ay, Lords of the Main—
The first-born of Neptune are Lords of the Main.

Nor are we alone in the noble career;
  The *Soldier* partakes of the generous flame:
To glory he marches, to glory we steer;
  Between us we share the rich harvest of fame.
    Recorded on high,
    Their names never die,
Of heroes by sea and by land what a train!
    To the *King*, then, God bless him!
    The *World* shall confess him
'The Lord of those men who are Lords of the Main.'
  Lords of the Main—ay, Lords of the Main—
The Tars of Old England are Lords of the Main.

                        LIBERTY.

LIBERTY.

["The following piece" fays Rivington's Royal Gazette, No. 352, February 12th, 1780, "is fuppofed to be written by a Loyalift without the lines." There is fatiffactory evidence, however, that Mr. STANSBURY was its author.]

WHEN at firft this land I preft,
  Pleafing rapture fill'd my breaft;
Swains in carols fweet and free
Sung the praife of Liberty.
Now their Halcyon days are o'er;
Fled to fome more happy fhore.
There, from civil Difcord free
Dwells the Goddefs Liberty.

At Bellona's harfh alarms
Simple yeomen fhine in arms.
Brother flain by brother, fee !
Dreadful fruits of Liberty.
Law and order proftrate lie;
Commonwealth is all the cry.
Tho' we flaves at prefent be
'Tis all for glorious Liberty.

What tho' Commerce droops her head,
All her fons to deferts fled:
Let's to *Clinton* bow the knee;
We're fecure of Liberty.
Wealth propitious fwells our ftore;
All our Coffers running o'er;
Dollars cheap as dirt fhall be.
Who wou'd not fight for Liberty?

Splendid

Splendid honours I difdain:
Crowns of Kings are lin'd with Pain.
Friendfhip only give to me,
Social joys, and Liberty.
Let me in my humble fphere
Free from envy, free from care,
Spend the days allotted me
Bleft with Peace and Liberty.

FREEDOM.

[Collated from two verfions in the Manufcripts of Mr. STANS-
BURY, and dated March 5th, 1780. It is hardly neceffary to add
that the fong is ironical.]

TO Freedom raife the lofty fong.
   Sublimeft joys to her belong.
'Tis fhe that fmooths the face of War;
Hides with laurel ev'ry fcar.
Huzza for the bleffings of Freedom, oh!

To her we owe, that fix'd as fate
Appears our independent State;
Our crowded ports and growing trade;
Honours too, which ne'er fhall fade.
Thefe, thefe are the bleffings of Freedom, oh!

'Tis She produc'd thofe wife and great
And honeft men who rule the State;
To meaner trades no more confined—
Awls and handfaws left behind—
How great are the bleffings of Freedom, oh!

Some

Some wretches may difgrace the Caufe
(For human nature's full of flaws)
And filch away the public wealth:
Speculate — by way of ftealth —
Difgracing the banners of Freedom, oh!

The Tories cry our Paper down;
Count forty dollars but a crown:
For which we'll tax and plague them more
Than Pharaoh's flaves in days of yore;
And all for the honour of Freedom, oh!

Then fill the glafs to Fredom, oh!
Fill up the glafs to Freedom, oh!
May the prefent conteft hold
Till my Paper's turn'd to Gold—
Then, a fig for the battle for Freedom, oh!

ON ADMIRAL ARBUTHNOT.

A PASQUINADE STUCK UP AT NEW YORK, AUGUST 12TH, 1780.

[This piece is attributed to Mr. STANSBURY, and is a fair example of the manner in which the inertneſs of the Engliſh leaders was criticized by the loyaliſts. It is preſerved in the Political Magazine, vol. II, p. 291 (London, May, 1781). It refers to the failure of Sir Henry Clinton's plan of an attack on the French fleet and troops lately arrived at Rhode Iſland by a co-operation of the Britiſh land and naval forces from New York.[76]]

OF Arbuthnot, my friend, pray tell me the news;
   What's done by his ſhips and their brave gallant crews?
Has the old Engliſh man ſhewn old Engliſh ſpunk
And the ſhips of the French burnt, taken, or ſunk?

In truth, my good ſir, there has been nothing like it.
'Tis eaſier to threaten a blow, than to ſtrike it.
No ſhip has been taken, or frigate, or lugger:
Nor e'en a poor Frenchman for jacktars ———
Though this was a promiſe ſo ſolemnly made
When he call'd on the ſailors to give him their aid:
Yet himſelf he has hid under Gardiner's Iſland,
And ſwears the French ſhips muſt be now taken *by* land.

A PASQUINADE.

STUCK UP AT NEW YORK ON THE 25TH OF AUGUST, 1780.

[By STANSBURY; preserved in 11 Political Magazine, 291. "The rebels were then carrying off forage, and burning houses in sight of General Clinton."]

  HAS the Marquis la Fayette
   Taken off all our hay yet?
Says Clinton to the wise heads around him:
  Yes, faith, great Sir Harry,
  Each stack he did carry,
And likewise the cattle—confound him!

  Besides he now goes
  Just *under your* nose,
To burn all the houses to cinder.
  If that be his project,
  It is not an object
Worth a great man's attempting to hinder.

  For forage and house
  I care not a louse;
For revenge let the loyalists bellow.
  I swear I'll not *do* more
  To keep them in humour,
Than play on my violencello.

Since Charles Town is taken,
'Twill sure save my bacon:
I can live a whole year on that fame, Sir.
    Ride about all the day;
    At night, concert or play;
So a fig for those men that dare blame, Sir.

    If growlers complain
    I inactive remain,
Will do nothing, nor let any others;
    'Tis sure no new thing
    To serve thus our King;
Witness Burgoyne and two famous Brothers!

A POETICAL EPISTLE

FROM JOSEPH STANSBURY TO HIS WIFE.

[Printed from the original Manuscript, which is dated 'Saturday night, 23rd December, 1780.' From the tenor of these lines, we may infer that Stansbury had come to Philadelphia, and was waiting permission from the President and Executive Council of Pennsylvania to return to New York. The jocular reference to the cause of delay may relate to Francis Hopkinson, Judge of Admiralty, and the only Judge at the time, who was also known "as a Wit and a Poet beside," in the city. Mr. Hopkinson's witty *Letter on Whitewashing* may also be alluded to.]

MY Dear,
  You'll not wonder I'm almost in vapours!
This merciless, graceless detention of Papers—
When my head and my heart were as light as a Cork,
With the hope of a safe and quick passage to York—
Is almost too much for a Mortal to bear!
But Prudence suggests we should never despair;
And Reason points out that Good Humour and
  Patience
Are better Companions than half our Relations;
Take off the rough edge of illnature and malice
And make our dark Prison as gay as a Palace.

Tho' kept in suspense, yet, my dear, don't pronounce ill
Of President's views, or intentions of Council.
Such baseless opinions I'm sure you will alter
When once you reflect that a hugeous Defaulter,
A Judge, and a Wit, and a Poet beside,
For some small Offences this day has been tried.

Small Offences! you cry—yes, my dear—and with
 reason:
For Bribery's nothing compared with Treason.
And what was this bribe? Why, a glass of good Wine,
Which all men in office should have when they dine.
Whether paid for when bought, or a month or two after,
Might furnish the court with a subject for laughter;
Which Judges and Council, a pack of sly elves,
Most wisely determin'd to keep to themselves:
Afraid lest the Secret should 'scape thro' the key-hole,
The method of changing a Black to a Creole—
Or, if the comparison is not too trite,
The Secret of making a Blackamoor white!

A Cause so important has made me lose one day; }
Tomorrow must follow, because it is Sunday;   }
And Heav'n only knows what will happen on Monday. }

These Rhymes would scarce pass in a Ring for a Posy;
Yet, please to accept them, as coming from *Josey*.

INVITATION.

INVITATION.

[By Joseph Stansbury, then at New York. Printed from the original Manuscript, which is dated January 10th, 1781. These lively lines contain some covert satire on the royal leaders, and the encouragement they then bestowed on worthless seceders from the American Cause. A class of arrivals not enumerated, however, by the poet, is described in the Manuscripts of one of his friends, also a refugee at this period in New York.—"Our little half-demolished town here seems crowded to the full, and almost every day produces fresh inhabitants. Two or three days ago, five or six waggon loads of women and children were sent in from Albany, in imitation of the prudent policy of Philadelphia. It was impossible to see them without pain, driving about the streets, in the forlorn attitudes which people fatigued with travelling and riding in waggons naturally fall into, making fruitless searches for their husbands and their fathers."]

YE Members of Congress and Councils of State,
   By Rebellion who hope to become rich and great;
The project, tho' bulky, is lighter than Cork,
Then quit it in time, and come hither to York.

You'll here see an Army polite and well-fed;
And crowds of fine folks, who lay three in a bed;
With Ladies too wise to be shut up in Cloisters,
Or live upon Pulse, when there's plenty of Oysters.

If Musters, Fines, Taxes, improv'd beyond reason,
Or loyal attachment transformed to Treason,
Have wasted your Means or your Patience, come all
Where you'll pay, *for the present*, no Taxes at all.

But

But firſt load a Veſſel with lumber, and ſend her :
'Tis true ſhe may meet with ſome Man of War's
    Tender.
My *Shelah* fell in with the *Savage* and *Triton ;*
They ſold her, and left me the ſubject to write on.⁷⁷

If Loyal, come freely—if Rebel, come too ;
Only come *without* leave, it is all you've to do.
Take the Oath, and declare you was forc'd to this puſh ;
And if *York* will not ſuit you, repair to *Flatbuſh*.⁷⁸

You'll there find a country in which you may thrive ;
And two dollars, from you, will go farther than five
From a poor Refugee : and the reaſon is clear—
' It is good to provide leſt the Rebels come here.'

Here plenty of all things for Caſh may be had ;
If that ſhould be wanting, your caſe will be bad.
Yet Money's ſo plenty, you'll find, to your coſt,
That Gold, like your Paper, its value has loſt.⁷⁹

Should Fortune deny you a Mattraſs or Bed,
Or a Cloſet or Hovel to ſhelter your head ;
Conceal your chagrin, and a Volunteer enter,
And ſwear you came here Life and Fortune to venture !

If this ſhould not ſuit you, you may if you pleaſe
Join freely with loyal and brave Refugees,
And plunder your Friends and your Foes, great and
    ſmall ;
And if you are caught, why—they'll hang you, that's
    all.

They'll

They'll hang you, that's all—I repeat it again :
And that, you'll confeſs, puts an end to your pain.
'Tis what you are uſed to—but *here*, by the Lord!
Theft, rapine and murder may ſmile at the Cord.

But, joking apart, all the difference I find
'Twixt this place and that I left lately behind ;
I lie down in *peace*, and in *ſafety* ariſe,
And *Liberty's* mine, an invaluable prize.

So here I enjoy, with unſpeakable pleaſure,
The objects for which ſo much bloodſhed and treaſure
Have idly been waſted by both ſides, I fear :
And all who would taſte them, ſhould wiſely come here.

If all in Rebellion would take this advice,
The rupture ſo wide would be cloſ'd in a trice.
Forgetting paſt Quarrels we'd happily ſing,
Hearts and voices united, *O God Save the King!*

ODE

FOR THE ST. GEORGE'S SOCIETY AT NEW YORK.

[By Mr. Stansbury: written in 1781, and printed from his Manuscript.⁸⁰]

IN early Time, e'er infant Law
    From Wisdom's bed
    Had rear'd her head,
The tyrant kept his slaves in awe.
    Justice feebly pois'd the scale:
    Wisdom only could prevail.

In vain the aged Matron weeps
O'er blushing Beauty's rifled charms;
Her eyes on Heaven in vain she keeps:
The fainting Virgin fills the Robber's arms.
Secure he riots o'er his helpless prey,
Mocks all her woes, and bears the prize away!

Now brighter days began to dawn.
Oppression saw the light, and fled:
In dark Cocytus plung'd her head
    Beneath the infernal wave.
Fair Freedom gilt the spreading Lawn;
Her sons confess a generous flame:
Each ardent Hero pants for fame,
By gallant deeds to build a deathless name,
    Or fill a nobler grave.
Immortal Glory high in air
The heavenly standard spread!
    The laurel Wreath,
    The marble Bust,

The trophied canvaſs, and ſweet Clio's page
  Defy, O Time, thy utmoſt rage.
    The good and juſt
    Her ſpirit breathe.
'Tis Glory fires the Hero's prayer,
And crowns th' heroic dead.

  Swift at her call in every clime
  Her ſons appear in Virtue's cauſe;
  Valour ſupplied the force of laws,
  And raiſ'd their fame ſublime.

  'Twas thus great George our Patron ſhone.
  No Virgin then was heard complain:
  No injur'd Matron ſued in vain:
  To diſtant lands his fame was known.

  The friend of Man, the Tyrant's foe,
  His boſom felt a generous glow
      To ſuccour the diſtreſt:
  To lateſt times are handed down
  His gallant deeds, his juſt renown:
      And make his Memory bleſt.

  In honor of his natal day,
  His Sons their annual homage pay
      And emulate their Sire.
  Nor ſhall their grateful tribute end,
  Till final peals the Heavens ſhall rend
      And wrap this Earth in fire.

A

A SONG

FOR ST. GEORGE'S DAY, 1781.

T UNE : *The King's Old Courtier.*

[Written by STANSBURY at New York, and printed from his Manuscript.]

ON this day our Countrymen, ages before ye,
    Have sung of St. George, long remember'd in story,
The Patron of England, resplendent in Glory.
    Then Huzza for St. George and Old England!
    St. George and Old England, huzza!

Some Wits have pretended that George, like old Dagon,
Had little of Courage and Glory to brag on;
Himself a tame Priest, and a Faction the Dragon.

And *Dick*, of good fellows the pride and the life,
Imagined, to keep up the whimsical strife,
St. George was a Bully—the Dragon his Wife.

Tho' this explanation may now raise your laughter,
Could he punish a Wife, he can punish a Daughter,
And all his bad Children, we'll show you hereafter.

He can punish his children connected with France,
Who exulting Rebellion's striped Standard advance:
Repenting they soon must submit to his Lance.

                              And

And when to their Duty recover'd again,
And humbled the Pride of France, Holland and Spain,
His Flag spread in triumph shall govern the Main.

Then Clinton and Rodney and all gallant Souls,
Whose zeal for their country her fortune controuls,
On this day we'll honour with full flowing Bowls.

And while of St. George with fresh ardour we sing,
We'll pledge his great Namesake, our patriot King,
And loud with his Praise may the Universe ring.
    So huzza for St. George and Old England!
    St. George and Old England, huzza!

ON THE REVIVAL OF THE CHURCH-AND-KING CLUB.

NEW YORK, FEB. 21ST, 1781.

[From the Manuscripts of JOSEPH STANSBURY.]

WHEN a vile rebel band from Britannia's strong hand
    Would fain pluck the Sceptre and Ball,
For our Church and our King we will fight or we'll sing;
    And with them we will stand or will fall.
        Then come let us play,
        And keep holiday
        To celebrate Church and King.

A Club so renown'd, with such choice Spirits crown'd;
    Where honour and humour attend;
Should not flag or decay while the Sun rules the day,
    Nor till Time his long journey shall end.

Thus united we'll meet, while our Army and Fleet
    The fame of old England advance;
Till from East to the West we stand victors confest
    O'er the Congress, the Spaniards and France!

When that æra arrives, with our Sweethearts and Wives
    In Chorus we'll joyfully sing
A hymn to sweet Peace; may her blessings increase,
    And surround both the Church and the King!
        Oh, then how we'll play,
        And keep holiday,
        To celebrate Church and King!

                      SONG

SONG

FOR A VENISON DINNER AT MR. BUNYAN'S: NEW YORK, 1781.

[By STANSBURY: collated from two Manuscript copies. This piece was apparently written on occasion of an arrival of fresh provisions from beyond the British lines.[81]]

FRIENDS, push round the bottle, and let us be drinking
While Washington up in his mountains is slinking.
Good faith, if he's wise he'll not leave them behind him,
For he knows he's safe nowheres where Britons can find him.
When he and Fayette talk of taking this city,
Their vaunting moves only our mirth and our pity.

But tho' near our lines they're too cautious to tarry,
What courage they shew when a hen-roost they harry!
Who can wonder that Poultry and Oxen and Swine
Seek shelter in York from such Valour divine;
While Washington's jaws and the Frenchman's are aching
The spoil they have lost to be boiling and baking.

Let Clinton and Arnold bring both to subjection,
And send us more Geese here to seek our Protection.
Their flesh and their feathers shall meet a kind greeting:
A fat Rebel Turkey is excellent eating:
A Lamb fat as butter, and white as a Chicken—
These sorts of tame Rebels are excellent picking.

Today

Today a wild Rebel has smoaked on the Table:
You've cut him and slic'd him as long as you're able.
He bounded like Congo, and bade you defiance;
And plac'd on his running his greatest reliance.
But Fate overtook him and brought him before ye,
To shew how Rebellion will wind up *her* Story.

Then chear up, my lads: if the Prospect grows rougher,
Remember from whence, and for whom 'tis, you suffer:
From Men whom mild Laws, and too happy Condition,
Have puffed up with Pride and inflam'd with Sedition:
For George, whose reluctance to punish Offenders
Has strengthened the hands of these upstart Pretenders.

THE

THE ROYAL OAK.

[By Joseph Stansbury: printed from his Manuscript, dated May 2nd, 1781.⁸²]

WHEN Britain first, at Heaven's supreme command,
  Emerging rose from out the azure main;
This was the Charter of the favour'd Land,
  And crouds of Guardian Angels sung this strain:
    Secure while Ocean roars around your chalky shores,
    Thy Genius shall defy each hostile stroke;
    The Fates for you ordain the empire of the Main,
    And Glory hovers over your Walls of Oak.

The Oak, an emblem of your future fame,
  Abides unmov'd the elemental strife;
And one day shall acquire a glorious Name
  By shielding in his arms great Charles's life.
    Then filling earth and skies your mighty deeds shall rise:
    No nation then shall dare your rage provoke.
    From the East unto the West, to Neptune's Sons confest,
    The world shall bow in homage to the Royal Oak.

Then shall the long expected day appear
  When Britain's King shall be as good as great;
Rever'd by Foes, and to his People dear;
  The Friend and Father of a mighty State.
    Yet Faction in his days her hydra-head shall raise,
    And wrap her spotted Carcase in a Patriot's cloak:
    But Clinton on the shore shall banish'd Peace
      restore,
    And Arbuthnot rule the main in the Royal Oak.

Arbuthnot, train'd for half an age to war;
  To face death and danger where glory points the way;
And, often borne on Victory's beaming car
  Enjoy'd the triumph of the well-fought day—
    May he with vengeance fall on the perfidious Gaul,
    And strew their pale-faced Lilies o'er the main;
    That, as they run away, D'Astouche himself shall
      say,
    " Begar, me n'engage pas *Royal Oak* again!

                              WOODLANDS.

WOODLANDS.

[Printed from Mr. STANSBURY's Manuscript copy. Whence its title the editor cannot say. It is dated December 24th, 1782, at which period Stansbury must have been in New York, and could not therefore have written this piece at the Woodlands on Schuylkill, the seat of a brother tory, Mr. William Hamilton.]

WHEN Terror to Madness had near work'd the brain,
How sweet to return to cool Reason again!
To find that our hopes in our Country were just:
That Subjects with George might their Liberties trust.

Now Time from the eyes of the Vulgar has drawn
Burke's fine cobweb reasonings—those curtains of lawn.[83]
The Man of the People the People despise,
As children those Toys which a moment they prize.

When Rodney the lucky with his Seamen brave
Stood forth like true Britons their Country to save;
The conquest to Neptune so pleasing was found,
Their temples with Laurel and Seaweed he crown'd.

And now brighter prospects are spread to our view;
Fresh honour presaging this Year that is new;
Indulge we the hope War its horrors may cease,
And all Men enjoy soon the Blessings of Peace.

When

When Peace shall return here, and bring in her train
Eafe, Love, Joy, and Plenty, to brighten the Plain:
The Sword and Spear be to *Ares* refign'd,
And the Plough, Loom and Sail then fhall comfort mankind.

Foul Faction and difcord no more fhall be known;
But Love, Pity and Kindnefs fhall fit on a throne
To which all around us fhall joyfully bend,
And Peace crown our fhores till the World's at an end.

A CHRISTMAS SONG

FOR 1782.

[By STANSBURY: printed from the original Manufcript. The verfe alluding to Carlton and Wafhington, under the names of Guy and Hannibal, feems to have been defigned for obliteration by the poet.]

NOW that Chriftmas-time is come,
 Sound the Fife and beat the Drum:
  We'll live cheerily,
  We'll fing merily,
Now that Chriftmas-time has come.

Be the future Peace or War,
We're refolv'd to banifh Care:
  We'll lay forrow by,
  And tomorrow try
Whether it be Peace or War.

Why should we our moments lose
For a choice we cannot chuse?
  Since we cannot tell
  Guy or Hannibal
Conquer will—no moments lose!

Life, by Fear and Care destroy'd,
Longest seems when most enjoy'd.
  Let us live a day;
  And not give away
What by Care is soon destroy'd.

Hope her brightest banner spreads:
Victory dazzles o'er our heads:
  Britain rises high,
  Rebel Prizes fly;
Now, while Hope her banner spreads.

Soon shall Congress, France, and Spain,
Wish themselves in Port again;
  While the Dutchman's fate
  Makes him cry too late;
Curse on Congress, France and Spain!

Fill your Bumpers, charge them high:
Britain's name shall fill the sky!
  Prone her foes be hurl'd:
  Peace she'll give the world:
And her Fame shall never die!

LET US BE HAPPY AS LONG AS WE CAN.

A Song.

[Printed from the original Manuscript of JOSEPH STANSBURY, and evidently adapted to the situation of the tory refugees at New York, during the latter part of 1782 and the commencement of 1783, when the prospect was daily growing stronger of Great Britain relinquishing the War. In this juncture many of the loyalists foresaw the difficulties attendant on their choice of a future place of abode, when the protection of the king's troops should be withdrawn.]

I'VE heard in old times that a Sage us'd to say
  The Seasons were nothing—December or May—
The Heat or the Cold never enter'd his Plan;
That all should be happy whenever they can.

No matter what Power directed the State,
He look'd upon such things as order'd by Fate.
Whether govern'd by many, or rul'd by one Man,
His rule was—be happy whenever you can.

He happen'd to enter this world the same day
With the supple, complying, fam'd Vicar of Bray.
Thro' both of their lives the same principle ran:
My boys, we'll be happy as long as we can.

Time-serving

Time-serving I hate, yet I see no good reason
A leaf from their book should be thought out of season.
When kick'd like a foot-ball from Sheba to Dan,
Egad, let's be happy as long as we can.

Since no one can tell what tomorrow may bring,
Or which side shall triumph, the Congress or King;
Since Fate must o'errule us and carry her plan,
Why, let us be happy as long as we can.

Tonight let's enjoy this good Wine and a Song,
And relish the hour which we cannot prolong.
If Evil will come, we'll adhere to our Plan
And baffle Misfortune as long as we can.

GOD

GOD SAVE THE KING.

[Collated from two Manuscript versions and written by Mr. STANSBURY, at New York but a short time before the end of the war.]

TIME was, in defence of his King and the Right,
  We applauded brave Washington foremost in
      fight:
On the banks of Ohio he shouted lustily
            God save the King!
Disappointed ambition his feet has misled;
Corrupted his heart and perverted his head:
Loyal no longer, no more he cries faithfully
            Glory and joy crown the King![84]

With Envy inflam'd 'tis in Britain the same;
Where leaders, despairing of virtuous fame,
Have push'd from their seats those whose watchword
      was constantly
            God save the King!
The helm of the State they have clutched in their grasp
When American Treason is at its last gasp:
When Firmness and Loyalty soon should sing valiantly
            Glory and Joy crown the King!

But Britain, with Glory and Conquest in view,
When nothing was wanted, but just to pursue—
To yield—while her Heroes chanted triumphantly
            God save the King!
With curses consign to the Furies his Name,
Whose Counsels thus cover'd his Country with shame!
Loyalists still will chant, tho' heavily,
            Glory and Joy crown the King.
                              Tho'

Tho' ruin'd fo deeply no Angel can fave:
The Empire difmember'd: our King made a Slave:
Still loving, revering, we fhout forth honeftly
    God fave the King!
Tho fated to Banifhment, Poverty, Death,
Our Hearts are unalter'd, and with our laft breath
Loyal to George, we'll pray moft fervently
    Glory and Joy crown the King!

THE UNITED STATES.

[Thefe lines, by Mr. STANSBURY, are written on the back of his *God fave the King.* Their date is probably about that of the recognition by England of our independence.]

NOW this War at length is o'er;
 Let us think of it no more.
Every Party Lie or Name,
Cancel as our mutual Shame,
Bid each wound of Faction clofe,
Blufhing we were ever Foes.

Now reftor'd to Peace again,
Active Commerce ploughs the Main;
All the arts of Civil Life
Swift fucceed to Martial Strife;
Britain now allows their claim,
Rifing Empire, Wealth, and Fame.

TO CORDELIA.

[These lines were addressed to his wife by Mr. STANSBURY from Nova Scotia; whither at the close of the Revolution he had retired with many other tory refugees. They are printed from a manuscript copy collated with a version published at Philadelphia, in 1805, on page 140 of The Evening Fireside—a literary periodical chiefly supported among the Quakers.]

BELIEVE me, Love, this vagrant life
   O'er Nova Scotia's wilds to roam,
While far from children, friends, or wife,
   Or place that I can call a home
Delights not me;—another way
My treasures, pleasures, wishes lay.

In piercing, wet, and wintry skies,
   Where man would seem in vain to toil
I see, where'er I turn my eyes,
   Luxuriant pasture, trees and soil.
Uncharm'd I see:—another way
My fondest hopes and wishes lay.

Oh could I through the future see
   Enough to form a settled plan,
To feed my infant train and thee
   And fill the rank and style of man:
I'd cheerful be the livelong day;
Since all my wishes point that way.

But when I see a sordid shed
  Of birchen bark, procured with care,
Design'd to shield the aged head
  Which British mercy placed there—
'Tis too, too much: I cannot stay,
But turn with streaming eyes away.

Oh! how your heart would bleed to view
  Six pretty prattlers like your own,
Expos'd to every wind that blew;
  Condemn'd in such a hut to moan.
Could this be borne, Cordelia, say?
Contented in your cottage stay.

'Tis true, that in this climate rude,
  The mind resolv'd may happy be;
And may, with toil and solitude,
  Live independent and be free.
So the lone hermit yields to slow decay:
Unfriended lives—unheeded glides away.

If so far humbled that no pride remains,
  But moot indifference which way flows the
    stream;
Resign'd to penury, its cares and pains;
  And hope has left you like a painted dream;
Then here, Cordelia, bend your pensive way,
And close the evening of Life's wretched day.

NOTES.

NOTES.

Note 1, Page 1.

ALTHOUGH the date of this piece is anterior to the commencement of hostilities between England and America, its allusions to the "party contentions" which were already beginning to rage, may justify its insertion here. Of the author, Mr. JOSEPH STANSBURY, the editor is not able to give much information. He was an Englishman who had emigrated to America several years previously. The following verses were perhaps the first fruits of his Muse in his adopted land. They are given from a manuscript version collated with that printed in the Evening Fireside (Philadelphia, 1805), page 124; and purport to have been written by Mr. Stansbury on his arrival in Pennsylvania towards the end of the year 1767.

MY NATIVE LAND.

Borne by Eolus o'er the Atlantic waves,
    To Indian lands unknown I wayward stray,
Whose verdant bosom silver Schuylkill laves;
    Stately and silent as the close of day,
Where rears the lofty spire its gilded crest,
    And thriving Commerce drives the busy Car,
In solemn pomp, by liberal Nature drest,
    Majestic rolls the mighty Delaware.

'Tho'

Tho' foothing Friendship here her healing balm,
    From unexpected hands, benign bestows,
And o'er life's troubled surface spreads a calm
    Which lulls to silent rest my former woes;
Still painful Memory prompts the gushing tear,
    (Her retrospective mirror in her hand,)
When lively images of kindred dear
    Inspire the wish to see my native land.

Tho' manly health with each returning sun,
    Sheds choicest blessings on my favour'd head,
And when this busy varied day is done
    Still keeps his watchful station round my bed:
Yet still, beneath severe Reflection's power,
    The numerous past transactions present stand,
And Nature's strongest ties, each present hour,
    Urge me in vain, to hail my native land.

Tho' Wealth, the lordly power by all ador'd,
    Seems kindly to increase my little store;
And hardy Temperance with a frugal board
    Forbids pale dreary Want to haunt my door;
Yet will a gentle race of kindred dear,
    Like airy Shades, conjur'd by magic wand,
Arise in view, and force a briny tear,
    A tear of reverence for my native land.

Tho' here Religion, heaven-illumined Fair,
    Breathes free, by papal shackles unconfin'd;
Prompts from the inmost soul the vital prayer,
    Alone well-pleasing to the Eternal Mind:
Still in my troubled sight, forever dear,
    Of relatives appear a much loved band;
Nor can my eyes restrain the streaming tear,
    While thus they call me to my native land.

Nor can the tender solace of a wife
  The lov'd idea from my breast erase;
Tho' much the dearest treasure of my life,
  Adorn'd with every sweet, attractive grace.
The friendly forms beloved, forever dear,
  Still stand confess'd and beckon with the hand:
Adown my cheek fast flows the briny tear,
  While thus they call me to my native land.

Alike the prospect of an offspring moves
  Life's purple current gladdening thro' my breast:
The long-wish'd produce of our mutual loves;
  The sweetest semblance of a soul at rest.
Yet still impetuous gush spontaneous tears,
  Like heaven-directed Nile o'er Memphis' strand:
To Wisdom's calming courage, deaf mine ears:
  I pant impatient for my native land.

Say, for what new and kindly purpose given
  This wondrous impulse, when abroad we roam:
Did Fancy plant it? No, it is from Heaven
  That joy springs blooming round the thoughts of home.

'Tis this by Liberty inspir'd, adorns
  The brightest pages of historic truth,
While Asia's Chief his vanquish'd thousands mourns
  Before the ardour of the Spartan youth.

No wonder then distils the pearly tear;
  It streaming flows at Nature's high command:
The ties of kindred are forever dear,
  And dear the memory of my native land.

                                                Mr.

Mr. Stanſbury was probably a native of London. In 1785, his ſiſter, Mrs. Collins, reſided at St. Paul's Churchyard in that city. But, from the time of his arrival in America, he appears to have conſidered this country as his home. In Philadelphia he eſtabliſhed himſelf in trade; and by his commercial integrity, his literary taſtes, and his many private virtues, ſoon acquired the eſteem of moſt of the chief characters of the city. At a more advanced period his political opinions brought him into direct oppoſition to a number of his perſonal friends: but deſpite the ready wit with which he aſſailed the whigs and even the perſonal adherence that he gave to the royal ſtandard, he ſtill continued to command their good-will. "He uſed to rail without meaſure at the whigs, whom "he held in great contempt," ſays tradition, "but neverthelefs ſuch was his "amiability of diſpoſition and his ſocial worth that even by whigs of the "firſt ſtanding in politics and ſociety he was prized and eſteemed."

When the Britiſh occupied Philadelphia in 1777, Stanſbury was of courſe one of thoſe who remained to welcome Howe and his followers, in whom he viewed the reſtorers of civil order and the deſtroyers of rebellion. So far as can be gathered now, he had belonged up to a certain period, to the moderate oppoſition: diſſatiſfied with the miniſterial proceedings in regard to America, but totally averſe to a reſort to arms to procure redreſs. There was a large and influential claſs in Pennſylvania who took this view of affairs; and the Declaration of Independence in 1776, was a ſignal for the withdrawal of many (ſuch as the Allens and others) from the whig ranks, even after they had aſſociated in arms againſt England. They would reſiſt as Engliſhmen, not as Americans. By all who came under ſuch a category, the approach of the king's troops was of courſe gladly hailed. By reference to the local newſpapers of the day, we find that Stanſbury on the 10th October, 1777, removed his china ſtore to Front ſtreet, between Market and Cheſnut ſtreets; and that in the ſame month he was appointed by the royal general one of a commiſſion for ſelecting and governing the city watch. On Monday, May 4th, 1778, he was choſen a director of the Library Company of
Philadelphia;

Philadelphia; and on the 15th of the same month, his name is publifhed with thofe of feveral others of the leading citizens, as a manager of Howe's Lottery for the relief of the poor of the place. On the evacuation of the city, he probably accompanied the fleet to New York, where he continued to dwell during the remainder of the war. During all this period his pen was active in the caufe of Great Britain, nor did he always fpare the follies of her friends, while he condemned what he confidered the crimes of her enemies. All of his productions that can be identified by the editor, and have any political bearing, are given in the preceding pages: the following lines were omitted however in the body of this volume, becaufe though attributed to Stanfbury, the evidence of their authorfhip is purely conjectural. They were printed in Rivington's Gazette—Rivington's *Lying* Gazette, the Americans ftyled it—March 2d, 1782. Their occafion was the fubjoined Epigram, that appeared in the Freeman's Journal (publifhed by Francis Bailey at Philadelphia), February 13th, 1782, in regard to the title of Rivington's paper having been fo blurred in the printing as to be fcarcely legible. Rivington's firft name was James.

   Says Satan to Jemmy, I hold you a bet
   That you mean to abandon our Royal Gazette;
   Or, between you and me, you would manage things better
   Than the Title to print on fo damned a Letter.

   Now, being connected fo long in the Art,
   It would not be prudent at prefent to part:
   And People perhaps would be frighten'd and fret,
   If the Devil alone carried on the Gazette.

   Says Jemmy to Satan, (by way of a wipe)
   Who gives me the Matter fhould furnifh the Type.
   And why you find fault I can fcarcely divine,
   For the Types, like the Printer, are certainly thine.

              'Tis

'Tis your's to deceive with the semblance of Truth,
Thou Friend of my Age and thou Guide of my Youth!
But to prosper, pray send me some further supplies,
A Sett of new Types and a Sett of new Lies.

This effusion was subscribed M. The answer in Rivington bears the letter N: and is so inferior to Stansbury's usual standard that it can hardly be of his composition.

THE RETORT-COURTEOUS.

Says the Poet to Bailey, pray what is the Reason,
Since you so delight in printing our Treason,
That your paper is oft times so *soft* and so *blue*,
That we cannot tell *Tool* from *Fool*, or *I* from *U* ?

Says Bailey, the reason is plain, Master Poet;
Had you one grain of Sense you surely would know it.
Its softness resembles the sculls of my Writers,
Who're a Sett of nerveless insipid Inditers.

And tho' the Colour's unlike both Christian and Jew Skin,
Yet it greatly resembles a true Rebel *Blue-Skin:*
Besides the texture well suits such labours as thine,
Which even Minerva can't save from Clo'cine.

Perhaps the following extract, from a manuscript letter from a loyalist in New York to a friend in Philadelphia, may explain how the authorship of these lines was given to Stansbury. It is possible that Bremner was, for caution's sake, used for Bailey; and though the year in which the letter was written does not appear, yet it was certainly not remote from 1782. In reference to some enclosures he had received from Philadelphia, the writer, under date of Feb. 26th, says: "The German

paper

"paper pleaf'd feveral Heffian officers and the lines on Bremner feveral perfons of tafte. Stanfbury was charm'd with them, and Rivington is to ufher them into the world."

While in New York, Stanfbury preferved the friendfhip of his old friends among the loyalifts; and would even feem, in December, 1780, to have vifited Philadelphia. At the clofe of the war, he went to Nova Scotia with a view to fettling there on the lands affigned by England to the refugees; but the country feems to have found as little favour in his eyes as in thofe of William Cobbett, and he foon returned to the United States. Under date of November 14th, 1785, a lady at Philadelphia writes: "Jofeph Stanfbury called on us the other day: his fpirits and vivacity are ftill the fame. He propofes living in this city in the fpring: at prefent his family are at Moorestown in the Jerfeys, where he fays any body may live." But if the People at Moorestown were willing to forgive and forget, thofe at Philadelphia were not. On December 22nd, 1785, the manufcript laft quoted from fays: "Jofeph Stanfbury lives at Moorestown; but intended to have taken a ftore here and gone into the fame line of bufinefs as before. But a fortnight fince, when he was in town, a letter directed to him was thrown into a houfe where he was fuppofed to lodge. The purport of it was that he muft immediately leave this city, as he would not be permitted *to live* in it; and figned *Mulberry Ward*. His friend R. Wells advifes him to give up the idea of coming here at prefent, and go to Wilmington as a place of trade. Some warm people met the evening before the letter was fent and had fet in judgment on Jofeph's works; his *Town-Meeting* and fome other performances were read and did not tend to cool, but rather to warm; and produced the hint to depart. I fhould not have mentioned this affair but that I know fuch reports often go abroad with additions, and that it would be beft to relate it as it is. He is a very obnoxious character with fome people." From another fource I learn that he finally fettled in New York, where he paffed the remainder of his life.

Although there were others of his name in America before the war, it is not known whether they were of the same family with our author. On the 17th January, 1775, we find *D. Stansbury*, junior, one of the Committee of Observation (whig) for Baltimore county, Maryland; and the name yet exists in Baltimore.

With a very few exceptions, I am authorized to believe that the pieces presented in this volume do not give a fair estimate of Stansbury's genius. Although he wrote a great number of poems, &c., during the Revolution, but a small number are preserved; and these owe their safety rather to accident, or to the fact of their being already in print, than to his own inclinations. "He wrote much in the heyday of the Revolution that he "afterwards destroyed: for with him all resentments died at the close of "the struggle, and he even seemed to forget who had hated and who had "injured him. His friends he never forgot." The best authority that I can refer to on this point declares that most of his pieces collected in this volume were but the creatures of the moment, " Scarce a line of which "he would himself have remembered a day after the ink was dry." Nevertheless, since fortunate circumstances have enabled me to gather together pretty much all that is known to exist of Stansbury's writings, I cannot but esteem them worthy of preservation; often for their own decided merit, and in every case as significant memorials of the days gone by.

The only passage, in the Song that has occasioned this note, which may demand an explanation, is the reference in the fourth stanza to the dispute between England and Spain respecting the Falkland Islands. After all, Spain finally retained undivided possession of the worthless but disputed territory. John Adams's letter to his wife of 23rd April, 1776, contains some curious facts about the St. George's Society at Philadelphia at that day.

Note 2, Page 3.

The antecedents of many who, towards the crisis of war, became tories, or at least were opposed to taking up arms against England, are thus inveighed against in the Monitor, No. VIII, published at New York, November, 1775:

The

"The very men who have now luckily fallen into such a pleasant dream of loyalty and obedience, in the time of the Stamp Act were most of them 'patriots of distinguished note;' the most vociferous clamorers for liberty and property; the life and soul of mobs; the leaders in all the valorous expeloits of plebian phrenzy, such as parading the streets with effigies, pulling down houses, tarring and feathering and the like. In a word, they did not scruple in those days to run headlong into practices much more wanton and disorderly than any that have happened in the course of our present struggle, which has been managed with singular decency, regularity and prudence.

"They then thought it no treason, no mortal sin, no Republican or Presbyterian contrivance, to form a Continental Congress; to petition and remonstrate with spirit and freedom; to deny the right of taxation claimed and exercised by the Parliament; to enter into agreements for the restriction of commerce; to act in every respect with suitable vigour and resolution. They did not tremble at the sound of Ministerial vengeance; neither were they afraid to adopt any decisive measure, because it might tend to irritate, to widen the breach, to throw an obstacle in the way of peace and reconciliation, and the rest of the trite nonsense, the product of these exuberant times. The contracted views of party, the sordid motives of ambition and avarice, had not then taken such firm hold on their minds as they have since. They felt the force of reason, listened to its dictates, and coöperated in the necessary means of bringing speedy relief to their Country."

Since the above has been in the printer's hand, the editor has been favoured with some passages in reference to Stansbury, extracted from the Pennsylvania Records and Archives, which are subjoined.

On the 25th November, 1776, at a meeting at the Indian Queen, in Philadelphia, "Mr. Smith attended and informed that he thinks Joseph Stansbury sung *God Save the King* in his house, and a number of persons present bore him Chorus, on the 15th October, 1776," &c. For this offence, the singers were, it seems, forced to enter into obligations to con-

fine

fine themselves to their own dwellings: and they probably soon underwent a severer punishment. On December 10th, 1776, the Council of Safety ordered that an enquiry should be made into the causes of the commitment of Joseph Stansbury, William Smith, and others, and that the confirmation or annulment of their confinement should depend on their being found free from disaffection to the Whig cause, and on their taking the oath of fidelity and allegiance to America. On January 4th, 1777, this Council ordered £5 11s. 3d. to be paid Stansbury for glass and delph ware obtained for the Montgomery, a public ship. In the Minutes of the Supreme Executive Council these entries occur: " Phila-
" delphia, Nov. 27, 1780. Monday. *Ordered*, that Robert Smith, Esq.,
" Agent for Estates, do make out an inventory of the goods & effects in his
" possession, now or late the property of Joseph Stansbury, and make return
" to this Board immediately. * * * Dec. 13, 1780. A petition from
" Joseph Stansbury, praying to be permitted to retire within the lines of the
" enemy was read, and the same was rejected, so far as it respects his going
" to New York. * * * Dec. 18, 1780. On consideration, Ordered,
" That Joseph Stansbury, with his family, be permitted to go to New York,
" he giving his promise upon honour to proceed immediately to that city,
" and use his utmost endeavours to have Abijah Wright & Casper Geyer,
" now prisoners on Long Island, released and permitted to return home,
" and that he will not do anything injurious to the United States; that his
" effects be restored to him, & himself liberated as soon as he shall be ready
" to set out for New York; that the agent for confiscated estates be directed
" to deliver up the keys of his property. * * * January 8, 1781. On
" application, a pass was granted to Mrs. Stansbury (wife of Joseph Stans-
" bury), for herself, six children, and a servant maid, with her cloathing,
" bedding, &c."

NOTE 3, Page 5.

" May America prove a sure and lasting Asylum for the Liberties of
" Mankind!" (Author's note.)

Note 4, Page 5.

Of the hiftory of Dr. ODELL, the author of thefe verfes, I have very little to add to what is already given in *The Loyalift Poetry of the Revolution*, page 199. That he was the writer of *The American Times* (under the pfeudonym of Camillo Querno), printed in that work, is a fact of which I have now no doubt, although it is not there fo ftated, and although it has been attributed to the Rev. Dr. Myles Cooper. In the Royal Pennfylvania Gazette of 26th May, 1778, is a long piece in blank verfe entitled *America's Lamentation*, and fubfcribed C. Q. R.; which letters would more appofitely reprefent the name affumed by the writer of the *Times* than that of any other perfon connected with the tory prefs known to me. But this does not afford fufficient warrant for its introduction here. It opens thus:

> O Thou who, with furpaffing glory crown'd,
> Look'ft down from Albion's throne; the fole juft Lord
> Of this new world; to thee I'd fondly call;
> And with a filial voice ftill ufe thy name,
> O Sire, to tell thee how I love thofe beams
> That bring to my remembrance from what ftate
> I fell; how glorious once, under thy fhine, &c.

In regard to the proceedings againft Odell in the Provincial Congrefs of New Jerfey (fee *The Loyalift Poetry*, page 201), it may be added here that when charges were firft lodged with that body, he at the fame time (Oct. 13th, 1775) prefented a prayer that his cafe might be heard that day. He was in attendance on the houfe, and was paroled to return on the 17th; when after a hearing, it was refolved in fubftance that although his intercepted letter expreffed his oppofition to the whig proceedings, yet as that congrefs did not wifh to violate the right of private fentiment, and the letter not appearing to have been defigned to influence public

public meafures, *etc.*, they would pafs no public cenfure on him. He was afterwards more ftringently dealt with, in July and Auguft, 1776; doubtlefs in confequence of his connections with certain Britifh officers in June, as commemorated by himfelf in the *Birthday Ode* and the piece fucceeding it, *ante*, p. 7. The remainder of his life was chiefly paffed in New York and Nova Scotia. The manufcript of a loyal lady who mentions vifits from him at the former place on the 28th Oct., 1781, and 15th Feb., 1782, thus refers to his fettlement in the latter. "January 5th, 1785. " * * * Dr. Odell I fee is at his deftined abode, and really the Doctor's " profpects are very flattering. To hold three or four of the moft lucrative " offices in the Government is not always the lot of one perfon; which will " bring in £1000 *p. ann.*, and is a fituation beyond what he could expect. " I envy none their profpects in a new country. £100 in my native land " with my friends is worth £1000 elfewhere."

In addition to the poetical effufions of Dr. Odell already given, the following pieces may intereft the reader, although from their not poffeffing a political bearing they could not well be inferted previoufly. They are printed from manufcript copies, and now, it is believed, for the firft time. The fubjoined verfes were doubtlefs addreffed to the corps in which he had once ferved.

A WELCOME HOME TO THE TWENTY-THIRD REGIMENT

AFTER THE PEACE OF 1763.

From burning fands or frozen plains,
   Where Victory cheer'd the way,
Hail, ye returning, fmall remains
   Of many a glorious day!

In eight revolving years, alas,
   What havoc war has made?
A tear fhall fwell one circling glafs
   In memory of the Dead.

With

With English hearts, to fate resign'd,
  They earn'd a deathless fame:
For England bled, and left behind
  A sadly-pleasing name.

On many a widely distant land,
  Or in the howling deep,
Tho' now they seem by Death's cold hand
  Held in eternal sleep:

Yet are they far from what they seem;
  Their *clay* alone is cold:
The *soul*, a warm, etherial beam,
  No power of Death can hold.

This mortal frame is but a Screen
  Between us and the Skies;
Death draws the Curtain, and the Scene
  Then opens on our eyes.

'Tis we that *dream*, not they that *sleep:*
  Their hovering Spirits fly
Around you still, and on you keep
  A friendly watchful eye.

And thus the Chief, who lately led
  Your courage to the field,
May still be fancied at your head;
  Still warn you not to yield.

Your lost companions thus may strive
  With you each toil to bear:
May still in Fancy's eye survive
  Your future fame to share!

With joyful triumph, then, review
   Your toils and dangers paſt;
Fill up the circling glaſs anew,
   And—Welcome home at laſt!

Theſe verſes muſt alſo have been written during Odell's reſidence at London: the alluſions to Pope's works need no explanation.

ON POPE'S GARDEN AT TWICKENHAM: 1765.

Behold the conſecrated Bowers
   Where oft, with rapture ſweet,
The Muſe beguil'd the lingering hours,
   And cheer'd her Bard's retreat.

"To wake the Soul, the Genius raiſe,
   " And mend the Heart," he ſings:
Echo repeats the melting lays;
   And Fame her tribute brings.

Here nothing ſplendid, nothing great
   Your admiration claims:
No proud diſplay of wealth or ſtate
   Your envy here inflames.

No vain ſepulchral pomp is here;
   But every paſſing eye
Here pays the tribute of a tear,
   And every heart a ſigh.*⁎*

No breathing marbles do you meet
   Near this enchanting ſpot;
But Inſpiration holds a ſeat
   In yon Muſe-haunted grot.

⁎ A plain Obeliſk, to the Memory of Mrs. Pope, with this inſcription: *Ah Editha, Matrum optima, Mulierum amantiſſima, Vale!*

                                                         Delightful

Delightful Hermitage! where still
  Some nameless charm resides:
But ah! no more the murmuring rill
  Across the cavern glides.

The Genius of the grotto fled;
  And left the mournful stream,
No longer by the Muses fed,
  To vanish as a dream.

Yet here entranc'd a simple Swain
  With rapture seems inspired.
Here Fancy listens to the strain
  That first my bosom fired.

Methinks I hear in every tree
  The fluttering Sylphs around;
And lo! the ravish'd lock I see,
  A constellation crown'd!

Here, shelter'd by the solemn shade,
  The *Cloister* seems to rise,
Where *Eloisa*, hapless Maid,
  Still vents her tender sighs.

Here, shrouded in a bloody vail,
  A more ill-fated Fair
Glides by, and swells the hollow gale
  With shrieks of wild despair.

But hark? an *evangelic* song
  Reechoed from the Spheres,
Here floats the silver Thames along:
  " A God, a God appears!"

With awful and fublime delight
 'This hallow'd ground I tread;
Where Angels hover in my fight,
 And whifper o'er my head.

The next piece was evidently compofed during the ftorm of the revolutionary war.

MOLLY ODELL ON HER BIRTHDAY.

BY HER FATHER.

Amidft the rage of civil ftrife,
The orphan's cries, the widow's tears,
This day my rifing dawn of life
Has meafured five revolving years.

Unconfcious of the howling ftorm,
No figns of fhipwreck'd peace I fee;
For what, with all its buftling fwarm,
What is the noify world to me?

My needle and my book employ
The bufy moments of my day;
And, for the reft, with harmlefs joy,
I pafs them in a round of play!

And if, ere long, my vacant heart
Is to be fill'd with Care and Pain,
Still I fhall bravely bear my part
While Truth and Innocence remain.

With one more poem, this selection from Odell's miscellaneous manuscripts must terminate. The ensuing is chosen as partaking of an autobiographical character.

ON OUR THIRTYNINTH WEDDING-DAY;
6TH OF MAY, 1810.

Twice nineteen years, dear Nancy, on this day
Complete their circle, since the smiling May
Beheld us at the altar kneel and join
In holy rites and vows, which made thee mine.
Then, like the reddening East without a cloud,
Bright was my dawn of joy. To Heaven I bowed
In thankful exultation, well assured
That all my heart could covet was secured.

But ah, how soon this dawn of Joy so bright
Was followed by a dark and stormy night!
The howling tempest, in a fatal hour,
Drove me, an exile from our nuptial bower,
To seek for refuge in the tented field,
Till democratic Tyranny should yield.
Thus torn asunder we, from year to year,
Endured the alternate strife of Hope and Fear;
Till, from Suspense deliver'd by Defeat,
I hither came and found a safe retreat.

Here, join'd by thee and thy young playful train,
I was o'erpaid for years of toil and pain.
We had renounced our native *hostile* shore;
And met, I trust, *till death to part no more!*
But fast approaching now the verge of life,
With what emotions do I see a Wife
And Children, smiling with affection dear,
And think—how sure that parting, and how near!

The folemn thought I wifh not to reftrain:
Tho' painful, 'tis a falutary pain.
Then let this verfe in your remembrance live,
That, when from life releafed, I ftill may give
A token of my love; may whifper ftill
Some fault to fhun, fome duty to fulfill;
May prompt your Sympathy, fome pain to fhare;
Or warn you of fome pleafures to beware;
Remind you that the Arrow's filent flight,
Unfeen alike at noon or dead of night,
Should caufe no perturbation or difmay,
But teach you to enjoy the paffing day
With dutiful tranquillity of mind;
Active and vigilant, but ftill refign'd.
For our Redeemer liveth, and we know,
How or whenever parted here below,
His faithful fervants, in the Realm above,
Shall meet again as heirs of his eternal love.

The Infcription on Franklin's Stove was undoubtedly written by Dr. Odell. Independently of the affertion of his family, and the fact of a manufcript verfion in his handwriting, dated 1776, being now before me, abundant evidence of his authorfhip will be found in contemporaneous authorities. It is fo ftated in the Gentleman's Magazine for April, 1777; in Towne's Evening Poft; Philadelphia, Nov. 29th, 1777; in Bourcher's View of the American Revolution (London, 1797), p. 449; and in Rev. W. Smith's Works (Philadelphia, 1803), App. to Sermon on Franklin. But Judge Yeates, writing from Lancafter in December, 1777, attributes it to Mifs Deborah Norris; and a general tradition in Philadelphia afcribes it either to that lady, or her townfwoman Mifs Hannah Griffitts (See II Mems. Hift. Soc. Penn., pt. 2; p. 91); both of them of repute as authors. Nor were thefe the only fatiric verfes in which Franklin's lightning-rods figured. The reader will call to mind how

Peter

Peter Pindar rung the changes on the preference bestowed by George III and Sir Joseph Banks upon blunt over pointed conductors; the latter having been recommended by Franklin and the laws of nature as exclusively suitable for protection against electricity. And as for Odell's censure of Franklin's political course, it may, howsoever erroneous, be extenuated by the estimation in which the latter was held by as warm a whig as the former was a loyalist. In 1772, Arthur Lee wrote from London, to Samuel Adams, that Franklin (who was then in that city) was the tool and not the dupe of Lord Hillsborough's designs against the charter of Massachusetts. Several years after, Lee deliberately explains the circumstances under which he made that statement: "That he could be
" deceived as to the designs of the administration, I could hardly believe.
" That he was bribed to betray his trust I had not suspected. It remained,
" therefore, as the most probable conjecture, that he endeavoured to lull his
" constituents into security, that he might prevent any commotions which
" would hazard the lucrative posts he possessed. From whatever motive
" the deception sprang, the mischief of it was such as rendered a counter-
" action of it necessary. For that purpose, the following letter was written;
" but it was written in anger, and yet the experience I have had since
" would justify the worst interpretation of his conduct."—*Lee's A. Lee;*
1, 216, 257.

Note 5, Page 6.

In the absence of any authority of reference concerning Mr. Piercy, I am induced to add such notices of him as occur to my hand. He belonged to the methodist branch of the Church of England, and was one of the few of that class who opposed the cause of the crown. John Adams, then a delegate to the Congress sitting at Philadelphia, mentions him in his Diary under date of Sunday, Oct. 23rd, 1774: "Heard Mr.
" Piercy, at Mr. Sproat's. He is chaplain to the Countess of Hunting-
" don, comes recommended to Mr. Cary, of Charlestown, from her, as
" a faithful servant of the Lord; no genius, no orator." He afterwards

passed to the southward, and in February, 1778, is mentioned by Elkanah Watson *(Memoirs;* p. 53), as having been left by Whitfield in charge of the Orphan House at Bethesda, in Georgia. "We found the family of " Mr. Piercy highly refined and intelligent, and enjoyed their kind hospi- " tality with much interest. Meeting people of their cultivation and " delicacy in this remote and solitary abode, was the source to us of equal " surprise and gratification. The religious duties of the evening were per- " formed with great solemnity and impressiveness. At the ringing of a " small bell, the negroes, with their children, all came to unite with the " family in their devotions." Dr. Piercy was during the war a good deal in Charleston, preaching to and encouraging the American troops. Consequently, on the fall of the city in 1780, he was ordered to relinquish his clerical duties; and as his name does not figure among those of the "two hundred and ten most respectable inhabitants" who addressed Sir Henry Clinton in June, 1780, we may conclude that he took no pains to conciliate the new authorities. In this same year we find the "Rev. " Wm. Piercy, clerk," included as a rebel in the disqualifying act of the tory legislature of Georgia.

Passing to England, he soon managed to break with his ancient patroness, Selina, countess dowager of Huntingdon, as appears from one of his letters, dated Woolwich in Kent, April 3rd, 1784, now before me. He ascribes the cause to "the attempt to raise a new *Sect* or *Party*, " under her Ladyship's patronage, called by the fine name of *Seceders*, alias " *Self-created Bishops*. But as I did not chuse to expose myself to the just " contempt of all serious men of all denominations, I stand now totally " unconnected with her Ladyship: as she stands entirely unconnected with " dear Mr. Whitefield's places and all his people. This has so much dis- " pleased the Countess, that, with her great age and all together, she now " refuses to fulfill the solemn engagements made with me in the year ———; " which was to allow me an handsome salary as long as I was her minister " and chaplain abroad, together with full and honourable compensation for " One Hundred a year, settled on me for life, that I was under the necessity
" of

" of forfeiting on her account, when I firſt left this Kingdom. In one of
" the laſt letters which paſſed between us, ſhe informed me ſhe was on the
" point of giving up Bethefda to the States. Indeed, ſhe never will do
" anything ſatiſfactorily with it, ſo as to fulfill Mr. W.'s Will; ſo that, in
" every view, the State had better have it at once, than ſuffer the whole
" Eſtate and Charity to lay waſte."

Dr. Piercy ſubſequently returned to Charleſton, and in 1809-10 was preſſing his claim againſt Lady Huntingdon on the Bethefda property. "If you cannot obtain thoſe negroes for me, the ſole property of the " Counteſs," he writes, " I hope, beſides the ſpecific propoſition for £500, " you will try hard to obtain the ſpecific intereſt upon the note." In 1812 he returned to England, where he ſoon after died. It is told of Dr. Piercy that being called on by ſeveral of his congregation, during a period of exceſſive rains, to offer up in his church the accuſtomed prayer for fair weather, he replied, after conſiderable heſitation and thumbing of the almanac, that he would certainly do as they wiſhed; but that the whole experience of his miniſtry taught him that all the prayers in the world would be inefficacious to procure an alteration in the weather until the moon changed. For more concerning him ſee *The Life of Lady Huntingdon;* volume ſecond.

Note 6, Page 7.

This feſtivity is thus alluded to in the Diary of James Craft of Burlington, as publiſhed in the Hiſtorical Magazine, vol. 1; page 301: " 1776, 7 mo. 13. The Engliſh Priſoners, nearly 90 of 'em ſent off guarded by " 18 men. They came here about the 26th of 4 mo. laſt. They had " their Band of Muſick in the Iſland on the 4th of 6th mo. And that " had liked to have made a Rumpus." Probably Major (then Lieutenant Andre) was one of theſe. They were removed from Burlington, as being too nearly within reach of Howe, and ſent to the interior of Pennſylvania. Under date of July 14th, 1776, Marſhall's Remembrancer ſays: " Yeſter- " day came to town about eighty priſoners taken at St. John's, on their " way, it's ſaid, to Cumberland County."

NOTE

Note 7, Page 14.

Due allowance for the power of the poet's imagination muſt be made while reading his panegyric on Queen Charlotte and her "blooming heavenly line." Wolcott paints her majeſty as

———— a downright ſlop
Form'd of the coarſeſt rags of Nature's ſhop;

and greatly lamented that "fierce George Hardinge," her Solicitor, deterred him from doing fuller juſtice to her ſordid traits. As for the children of the king and queen, there was certainly nothing very "heavenly" in the minds and morals of ſome of them.

Note 8, Page 14.

The manner in which the Declaration of Independence was celebrated at the city where it was enacted and in the earlieſt years of the war, is a matter of ſome intereſt.

On the 5th of July, 1776, Congreſs ordered that copies of the Declaration ſhould be tranſmitted to the ſeveral Aſſemblies, Conventions, Councils of Safety, &c., that it might be properly proclaimed. On the 6th this Reſolve was received by the Philadelphia Council of Safety, which ordered "that the Sheriff of Philadelphia read, or cauſe to be read and proclaimed "at the State Houſe, in the City of Philadelphia, on Monday, the 8th day "July, inſtant, at twelve o'clock at noon of the ſame day, the Declaration "of the Repreſentatives of the United States of America, and that he "cauſe all his Officers, and the Conſtables of the ſaid City, to attend the "reading thereof." The Council likewiſe reſolved to attend the reading in a body, and to invite the Committee of Inſpection to be preſent. In the latter Committee it was, on the 6th, reſolved ſo to attend. "At the "ſame time, the King's Arms there are to be taken down by nine Aſſo- "ciators, here appointed, who are to convey it to a pile of caſks erected "upon the commons, for the purpoſe of a bonfire, and the arms placed

"or

"on the top." As the public election for members of the State Convention was to come off on the 8th, at the State House, this measure was opposed, left the election might thereby be disturbed, but it was carried in the committee by a majority.

Accordingly, on Monday, the 8th of July, 1776, "in the presence of "a great concourse of people, the Declaration of Independence was read "by John Nixon. The company declared their approbation by three "repeated huzzas. The King's Arms were taken down at the Court "Room, State House, at the same time. From there some of us went "to B. Armitage's tavern; stayed till one. I went and dined at Paul "Fooks's; lay down there after dinner till five. Then he and the "French engineer went with me on the commons, where the same was "proclaimed at each of the five Battalions. * * * Fine starlight, pleasant "evening. There were bonfires, ringing bells, with other great demon- "strations of joy upon the unanimity and agreement of the declaration."

On the night of Friday, July 4th, 1777—the first anniversary of our national jubilee—we are told by the Philadelphia newspapers of the time, that "there was a grand exhibition of fireworks (which began and con- "cluded with thirteen rockets) on the commons, and the city was beau- "tifully illuminated. Every thing was conducted with the greatest order "and decorum, and the face of gladness and joy was universal." Not a word is said in their news columns of any of those episodes that usually attend a civic illumination not entirely popular: and it was notorious that a very large part of the inhabitants, especially of the Quakers, were more or less secretly hostile not only to the principles but the measures of the party in power. The Friends in particular would not voluntarily give either passive or active encouragement to the orders of Congress; and had brought themselves into general notice by their refusal to comply with the recommendation for a General Fast, and suspension of business on the 17th May, 1776; by their murmurings against the new order of things; and by their indisposition to remove their effects from the city in December, 1776, when the threatened approach of Howe put all the whigs to

transporting

transporting their effects to places of safety. "The Friends here," says Marshall, "moved but little of their goods, as they seem to be satisfied "that if Gen. Howe should take this City, as many here imagined that "he would, their goods and property would be safe." To be sure there were many Friends who took up arms for America; but as these were almost all expelled from the Society for so doing, their conduct served only to make that of their old comrades more objectionable. Accordingly the celebration of the 4th of July, 1777, might reasonably have been expected to involve some local disturbances. The following letter from George Bryan, a distinguished whig, to his wife, will give some notion of the proceedings of the occasion.

PHILADELPHIA, 4th July, 1777.

My partner and friend:

It is now near eight in the evening. This has been a day of feasting and the anniversary of independence, which has, as such, been much noticed. I am just returned from dining with Congress at the City Tavern. * * * We have ordered out constables and watchmen, and expect two hundred soldiers to patrole, and that all illuminations and bonfires are to be put out at eleven this night. Perhaps some disorders may happen, but we were willing to give the idea of rejoicing its swing, The spirits of the whigs must be kept up.

One thousand Carolinians paraded under arms in Second street, and were reviewed by Congress and Generals Gates and Arnold. Two companies of artillery and a company of Georgian foot performed a *feu de joie*. The Maryland light horse attended and were reviewed. The gallies and ships came up and paid their compliments. I am, my dearest madam, your most devoted lover and partner and friend.

GEORGE BRYAN.

Mr. Bryan's anticipations were well-founded. Although, as has been suggested the local newspapers were perhaps under a too ominous pressure of whig bayonets to venture on publishing anything likely to injure the cause, there nevertheless appears, in the Philadelphia Evening Post of 5th July,

July, side by side with the " order and decorum " paragraph above quoted, an advertisement subscribed Daniel Humphreys, denouncing 'a banditti,' " headed by three certain persons " and a band of music, that had broken his windows, &c. On the 12th, Richard Peters in another advertisement replied to this statement; and assuming that himself and two others holding public employments under Congress were the "three certain persons" referred to, altogether denied his complicity. From all this, and from the passages to follow, it may be inferred that there was a pretty general assault upon the houses of such obnoxious characters in the city as refused to light up their windows on the night of July 4th, 1777. The newspapers contain nothing further on the subject; but the records of the Monthly Meeting of Friends at Philadelphia for the Southern District, 30th, 7th month (July), 1777, contain a report of the Committee "to " advise and assist such of our members who might be subjected to suffering " for the testimony of truth," which in a measure supplies the deficiency. "And likewise on the evening a day lately appointed by the present " powers for public rejoicing, divers Friends had their windows broken " by a licentious mob, because they could not join with the multitude in " illuminating their windows. But no account has been brought in by " any Friend of the loss or damage they sustained." And in the Northern District there is a similar record. In both, their blankets had been forcibly taken from them on a public requisition, " declared to be for fitting " out men to go to war." This was in consequence of the local authorities having appointed a committee to collect in the city and county of Philadelphia 1334 blankets for the army. The committee was empowered to direct the proportion to be taken from any family, on payment of an appraised value: but to such of the Quakers as would not receive Continental Paper Money, this payment was no great matter. " The being " compelled," continue the Quakers, " into a contribution for such a " purpose has been grievous to honest minds. And some have had their " stock of this necessary article so reduced, as to be likely to want the " needful covering in a cooler season." These trials they say they endure

" with

"with a good degree of patience and meekness;" and then recite the imposition of having soldiers billeted on them; their dwellings abused, and their windows broken, &c.; "because Friends could not illuminate "their houses, and conform to such vain practices, and outward marks of "rejoicing, to commemorate the time of these people's withdrawing "themselves from all subjection to the English government, and from an "excellent Constitution, under which we long enjoyed peace and prof- "perity."—*Almon's Remembrancer;* v, 292. *Gilpin's Exiles;* 294.

It was probably because of the troubles of this night that, the next year, Congress and the Council forbade any illumination at Philadelphia on July 4th, 1778; "on account of the excessive heat of the weather, the "present scarcity of candles, *and other considerations.*" The billeting of soldiers referred to above was probably that mentioned by Marshall, under date of January 25th, 1777: "Great quantities of backwoodsmen "coming to town this day: so many that with what were here before, "an order was issued for the billeting of them in the non-associators' "houses, which was put into execution in our part of the city." The non-associators were such as would not take up arms for America.

Note 9, Page 15.

Of General Gates and Judge Richard Peters, it can scarcely be necessary to say anything. The latter was born in 1744, and was during a great part of the revolution a member of the Board of War. He was always distinguished for his pleasantries; and acquired a more enduring reputation as a jurist during thirty-six years of service on the bench of the District Court of Pennsylvania, to which post he was appointed by Washington.

Note 10, Page 15.

James Meafe was born at Strabane, County Tyrone, Ireland; but came to Philadelphia before the commencement of the revolutionary troubles.

troubles. He was a warm whig from the outftart; one of the originators of the Firft City Troop, which did fuch good fervice at Trenton, and which has never fince loft its organization; and in 1777, Clothier-General of the American Armies. In 1780 we find him fubfcribing £5000 for the relief of the troops. In later years he did not efcape the fatiric lafh of Cobbett. See *Porcupine's Works;* XI: 246, 248.

NOTE 11, Page 15.

Richard and Thomas Willing, two prominent citizens of Philadelphia; one of them (Thomas) was a partner in the houfe of Willing and Morris, and of courfe connected with the extenfive undertakings for furnifhing fupplies to the army in which Robert Morris was fo largely engaged. The trait alluded to in the verfe to which this note refers is alfo recorded by John Adams in his Diary for Sunday, 11th September, 1774: "Dined at Mr. Willings. * * * A moft fplendid feaft again—turtle and "every thing elfe." There are few things in his Works more amufing than the furprife and pleafure which, at this period of his life, Mr. Adams exhibits at the ftyle of living he encountered in the colonies fouth of New England He rarely rifes from the table without chronicling its equipage with a particularity worthy of old Pepys himfelf; and though he was undoubtedly willing, as he faid, to fubfift at Braintree in the utmoft frugality; to "eat potatoes, and drink water," if the ftruggle for freedom fhould bring him to that neceffity, yet it is not probable that he would not prefer to live as he was living at the time (1774) he made this profeffion—going " to dine with fome of the nobles of Pennfylvania at four " o'clock, and feaft upon ten thoufand delicacies, and fit drinking Madeira, " Claret and Burgundy till fix or feven." At this period there was probably a confiderable difference between the eaftern and the middle colonies in their ftyle of living.

NOTE

NOTE 12, Page 15.

This paſſage relates to the Conſtitution of Pennſylvania framed in 1776 by a convention not regularly authorized ſo to do; yet under which the State was governed for ſeveral years. In his animadverſions upon it, the tory ſatiriſt has more reaſon than in moſt of his philippics. Graydon ſays that its principal authors were George Bryan and a ſchoolmaſter named James Cannon; though Dr. Franklin was ſuppoſed to have given either his aid or his countenance to their lucubrations; and tradition affirms that it was drawn up in a ſingle night. It is unneceſſary here to go into a recapitulation of its details. It muſt ſuffice to obſerve that it differed fundamentally from the form of government which it ouſted; and that it was bitterly oppoſed not only by the tories, the Quakers, and the "moderate men," but alſo by Cadwalader, St. Clair, Morris, and numerous others of the moſt diſtinguiſhed among the whigs. Its own limitations ſhut out for ſome time any change in its proviſions, and the whole power of the State was thus veſted in its friends. Thus John Adams, who was no admirer of it, thought it "agreeable to the body of the people;" yet he could not conceal the light in which it deſerved to be regarded. "The proceedings "of the late convention," he writes ſhortly after it had framed this conſtitution and diſſolved, "are not well liked by the beſt of the whigs. Their "conſtitution is reprobated, and the oath with which they have endeavored "to prop it, by obliging every man to ſwear that he will not add to, or "diminiſh from, or any way alter that conſtitution, before he can vote, "is execrated." It certainly had one good effect, in excluding from any political influence every inhabitant of the ſtate who was not in favour of the extreme meaſures of the party ſupporting Independence: but as it alſo excluded many who were in favour of that ſtep, and as it was, after all, tyrannical alike in its birth and in its adminiſtration, it was a wiſe proceeding to get rid of it as ſoon as poſſible. To be ſure ſeveral diſtinguiſhed characters, who were averſe to it at the commencement, in time accepted offices under it; but in ſuch caſes the purity of their motives muſt be weighed againſt the ſoundneſs of their judgment.

Note 13, Page 16.

This song refers to the following episode in our revolutionary history. As has already been remarked in a previous Note, the conduct of the Quakers of Pennsylvania was, in the earlier years of the war, extremely unsatisfactory to the whigs. Their willingness to remain at Philadelphia when the city was threatened by Howe in the winter of 1776-7, and when every one at all active on the American side was flying with his effects to the country, confirmed the suspicions already entertained against them. In March, 1777, John Adams writes from Philadelphia that " more than one half of the inhabitants have removed into the country, as " it was their wisdom to do. The remainder are chiefly Quakers, as dull " as beetles. From these neither good is to be expected nor evil to be " apprehended. They are a kind of neutral tribe, or the race of the " insipids. Howe may possibly attempt this town, and a pack of sordid " scoundrels, male and female, seem to have prepared their minds and " bodies, houses and cellars for his reception; but these are few, and " more despicable in character than number." And in the ensuing June, he again reverts to the impracticable indifference of the Quakers : " This town has been a dead weight upon us. It would be a dead weight " upon the enemy. The *mules* here would plague them more than all " their money." Mr. Adams had unfortunately for himself engaged in a logical controversy with some of the best informed among Friends on the questions of the day, and had not come out very triumphantly from the encounter. This may have embittered him against them. Accordingly in the latter part of the summer of 1777, when it was probable that Howe would speedily risk a pitched battle for the possession of Philadelphia, the wisdom of securing the persons of all such suspected characters as by wealth or social position might be able to be of assistance to him, presented itself seriously to the whig leaders. Some papers containing the proceedings of a Quaker meeting in New Jersey had fallen into the hands of General Sullivan, and by him were transmitted to Congress. These

documents

documents were sufficient to give an opportunity for the fulfilment of the wishes of many of the whigs; and it was resolved (August 28th) to request the Supreme Executive Council of Pennsylvania to forthwith apprehend eleven of the chief Quakers of the city, named in the resolution. The Council did as it was desired, and more. On the 9th of September, it ordered that twenty-three gentlemen named in the decree, should be removed to Staunton in Virginia and there secured. All of these were at the time in confinement at Philadelphia, and were generally Quakers; though there were some Church of England men among them. The allegation against them was that they had uniformly manifested a hostility to the United States; that they had refused to pledge their allegiance to the State of Pennsylvania and to promise to hold no correspondence with the enemy, and that they considered themselves subjects of the King of Great Britain. They were imprisoned, it was further said, because they would not promise to remain in their own houses while their case was under discussion.

These people endeavored to extricate themselves by *Habeas Corpus;* but the exercise of the writ was suspended so far as they were concerned. No expostulations which they would make, nor any effort to bring their case before a court of jurisdiction, availed them. They were dealt with in the spirit of martial rather than common law; and perhaps the exigencies of the times may have rendered a discreet exercise of such power advisable. Unfortunately however under the constitution of 1776 the control of the State was then mainly in the hands of the Presbyterians, between whom and the Quakers, and to some extent the Churchmen, there was a long-established political feud. This circumstance undoubtedly inspired vindictiveness on the one part and exasperation on the other. On the 8th of September, Adams thus writes from Congress: " You will
" see by the papers enclosed that we have been obliged to humble the
" pride of some Jesuits, who call themselves Quakers, but who love
" money and land better than liberty or religion. The hypocrites are
" endeavoring to raise the cry of persecution, and to give this matter a
" religious

"religious turn, but they can't succeed. The world knows them and
"their communications. Actuated by a land-jobbing spirit like that of
"William Penn, they have been soliciting grants of immense regions of
"land on the Ohio. American independence has disappointed them,
"which makes them hate it. Yet the dastards dare not avow their hatred
"to it, it seems."

In pursuance of the Order above mentioned, the prisoners in question, with others seized on a like ground, were exiled to Virginia and detained there for a very considerable period. Among those so treated was Benjamin Chew, formerly Chief Justice, of whom Thomas Lynch had written to Washington on the 13th November, 1775: "I am sure Mr. Chew is "so heartily disposed to oblige you and to serve the cause, that nothing "in his power will be wanting." Perhaps the arrest of some of the number was rather intended to prevent their doing future harm to the cause, than in punishment for any offence yet committed. Among the names included in the Order of Council is that of Thomas Wharton, *senior*. Thomas Wharton, *junior*, was President of the Council, and, as such, the Chief Executive Officer of the State. It was to him that the following characteristic letter was addressed by one of the prisoners, a gentleman of high standing in the city.

Hopewell, Virginia, March 9, 1778.—I could not have supposed that thou would have refused answering my letter merely on account of its wanting a little form. That this may not be neglected for the same reason, I now address thee under the title of (being only intended as a matter of form),

Friend Wharton,

Thee may remember that in the winter 1776 I and my son Isaac were dragged before the President and Council of Safety upon no other authority than the will and pleasure of a drunken Sergeant and his guard. On my return home I was very much affected with the thought that a person with whom I was formerly agreeably connected should be in a situation the most degrading of any I could conceive: It being evident

thou

thou waſt under the influence of this military guard. The next day I wrote thee a letter on the occaſion. Whatever then influenced thee not to return an anſwer, I dare ſay thou art now convinced it would have been better to have done it. Hadſt thou thought it worth while to have heard what I could have ſaid on the occaſion, it is probable I might have been uſeful to thee. With regard to our caſe, who have been condemned and baniſhed without trial; thoſe in authority have either not judged at all, leaving it to Congreſs to judge for them, or they have judged moſt unrighteouſly.

Notwithſtanding the account thee gives of thy time being taken up with thy father Fiſhbourne, &c., thou ſigned orders for our removal under eſcort of two of the Troop, dated Sept. 10th, and orders to Col. Morgan of the ſame date to look out for a proper perſon to convey us from Reading to Staunton; alſo a letter to John Hancock reſpecting our application to Council for our detention at Wincheſter, dated 12th of September.

From the above mentioned authentic papers, it is evident thou haſt been our enemy; and well might I ſay in my former letter that with regard to anything friendly, I am at a loſs in what manner to addreſs thee. But to take thee on the ground of inactivity, on which thou pretended to ſtand, but on which in reality thou didſt not—what would it amount to, but that thou would not commit the evil thyſelf, but keep out of the way, and let others do it? A baſe deſertion of the cauſe of the innocent and oppreſſed: but I have already ſhown thy crime is of a deeper dye.

Thou ſigned orders for our removal under eſcort of two of the Troop. Now what evidence hadſt thou againſt us, whereby thou wouldſt juſtify thyſelf in ſigning this decree? Did the general charge of the Congreſs, publiſhed in all the papers, againſt the people called Quakers, convince thee of our guilt? A moſt ſhameleſs performance, and which we could have fully anſwered in a ſhort time, had we been allowed our undoubted right of being heard in our defence. And now I put it to thy conſcience: what could induce thee to conſent to our being baniſhed for life? Thou couldſt not have believed we had been guilty of any crime that could deſerve ſuch puniſhment.

To

To complete this scene of iniquity, orders were issued from the War Office to our Conductors, not to suffer us to distribute our remonstrances. At the same time those charges made against us, published by order of Congress, were dispersed about with great assiduity. A remarkable instance of injustice.

A few words more, and I have done. Before thou signed this unjust decree, did it not occur to thee that thou wast well acquainted with a great number of us, and that thou knew us to be a quiet, peaceable people, that were by no means likely to be concerned in plots, or in giving intelligence to the enemy? But if any such thoughts took place in thy mind, it is evident they were not long cherished there. Thou signed the unjust, the cruel decree, without giving us an opportunity of being heard in our defence.

As it is impossible this conduct could proceed from the love of justice, so I think it is not possible thou canst enjoy peace in thy own mind until thou sincerely repents for the great injury thou hast done us, and makes us all the reparation in thy power. That thou mayest, through the assistance of Divine Providence, be enabled to witness a sincere repentance and amendment of life, is the desire of one who, when that event takes place, may with propriety subscribe himself thy real friend,

EDWARD PENINGTON.

In good sooth, any person seized on this occasion, whose conscience did not convict him, had great reason for indignation; but there was no ground for their fears who esteemed it a religious persecution, and in the mind's eye beheld

> Protestant Parsons whipp'd and scoff'd at,
> Quakers and Methodists thump'd and ston'd.

NOTE

Note 14, Page 16.

The power claimed before the war by the British Parliament, of transporting to England for trial persons charged with the commission of certain offences in this country; and of in many cases depriving the subject of the benefit of trial by jury; were especial American grievances, and are recapitulated as such in the Declaration of Independence.

Note 15, Page 17.

This passage again refers to the allegation that the revolt in the colonies was the work of the Presbyterians and their Congregational brethren in New England, and designed for their especial benefit.

Note 16, Page 17.

During its colonial existence, Pennsylvania had a paper currency to supply the necessities of its people; specie not being always sufficiently abundant. The bills were issued by virtue of acts of the legislature, approved by the crown and containing certain provisions for their redemption. They were loaned in various amounts to the inhabitants of the state on mortgage security, and thus readily went into circulation; and seem really to have been of great service to the community. When the continental paper bills however began to be issued, very many persons refused to receive them; and of course, on Howe's occupation of Philadelphia, their circulation was entirely prohibited. Such of the inhabitants, however, as adhered to the old order of things, and who had also, in all probability, accumulated a considerable sum in the Provincial (or as it was called *Legal*) Paper Money, saw no reason why this sort of currency should not continue in its former value. Some time elapsed after the British army was seated in the city before the fleet of men of war and of transports from New York, led by Admiral Lord Howe, could force a passage up the Delaware, which was for the period commanded by the American

American fortifications on the banks: and during this state of suspense, as nothing could be settled until Sir William Howe was in a condition to keep his communications with the sea open, the question of the circulation of Legal Paper Money remained undecided. When the fleet finally arrived, it brought quantities of goods to supply the exhausted markets of Philadelphia; and they who had the disposal of them at once declared they would receive nothing but gold and silver in payment. If it be true, as the poet urges, that " the merchant-stranger" perceived the improbability of Legal Paper Money ever being redeemed, because not only of the lands mortgaged for their redemption being chiefly in the hands of the whigs, but also by reason of the mortgage-deeds themselves being withdrawn; there was certainly good ground for their opinion. The citizens urged, on the one hand, that the bills were issued under laws sanctioned by the King; that they had long been the common circulating medium in the province; that their suppression would be alike disastrous to individuals, by destroying their only wealth, and to trade, by ousting the only medium adequate to its necessities; and that even the army itself would suffer, if all bills on England had to be paid for here in gold and silver. Their opponents, the storekeepers who came by the fleet, were equally persistent, and in the end prevailed. There is great reason to believe that Sir William Howe was secretly concerned with Coffin, one of the strangers mentioned in the text, and had a large share in his gains: and for this cause he may have been willing to discountenance a paper-money that would only be valuable so long as he himself was victorious.

In the piece to which this note relates, it would seem as though Stansbury had been willing to indulge in a little irony at the expense of his fellow loyalists, by versifying the language of a petition to Howe from some of the advocates for the restoration of the old paper currency, and at the same time interpolating the answers of its adversaries.

NOTE

Note 17, Page 18.

The year 1759 was diftinguifhed in America by the great fucceffes gained over the French by the Britifh. Ticonderoga, Niagara and Quebec were taken, and the way made clear for the downfall of French power in Canada.

Note 18, Page 19.

The accuftomed night-watch of the city was of courfe infufficient to preferve the peace on occafion of twelve or fifteen thoufand ftrangers being added to its population; and the firft days of Howe's occupation were marked by conftant thefts and burglaries. It was not confidered defirable to eftablifh a military patrol in place of a civil police ; fo Howe appointed a number of citizens to be Commiffioners of the Watch, and to increafe its numbers and efficiency. Of thefe Stanfbury was one. But as the men would not receive their pay in the paper money, which would buy them nothing in the fhops; and as the Commiffioners had no other to give them; there arofe an opportunity of bringing the matter before the Englifh General.

Note 19, Page 19.

This muft refer to an Addrefs of Congratulation to Howe on his arrival at Philadelphia, and to the refufal of people to fign it until he had fecured, fo far as in him lay, the value of their local currency by placing it, if not on a par, at leaft in a due proportion to fpecie as a legal tender.

Note 20, Page 19.

Faithful to their principles, the Quakers of Philadelphia were the only clafs there refolute not to be moved by the events of war. When Howe actually took poffeffion of the city in 1777, their conduct was fimilar to that which they difplayed in the preceding year when he threatened to
advance

advance upon it through the Jerseys. Robert Morris has vividly painted the scene on the latter occasion, in a letter to the Commissioners at Paris, dated Philadelphia, 21st December, 1776: "This city was for ten days " the greatest scene of distress that you can conceive: everybody but the " Quakers were removing their families and effects, and now it looks " dismal and melancholy. The Quakers and their families pretty gene- " rally remain," *etc.* On Howe's entrance in 1777, he issued a number of proclamations respecting the requirements of the army, the police to be maintained, and the like; a complete collection of which is now before me. One of them relates to the occasion of this Epigram, and as but one hundred copies of it were struck off for posting, and probably no other examplar exists, it is transcribed here at large.

" *Philadelphia, October* 31, 1777. Five or Six Hundred Blankets are " wanted for the Troops. The Inhabitants are requested to furnish that " Number to the Barrack-Master, who will pay for them, or return them " in a few Days." So soon as the fleet got up, it was doubtless an easy matter to restore blanket for blanket; but it is as easy to imagine that in such cases old lamps are generally exchanged for new. It is problematical whether Friends did not feel as sensibly the injury of being called on to supply blankets to the English soldiery as to the American: but they did not, at all events, complain of it so warmly.

Note 21, Page 20.

Many of the circumstances referred to in this Song, are related in a preceding Note. In order to bolster up the circulation of the paper money issued under the proprietary government, several hundred citizens of Philadelphia had subscribed an Agreement, dated October 1st, 1777, whereby they promised to take it at certain fixed rates: an English guinea to be estimated at thirty-five shillings, Pennsylvania currency, for instance; a Spanish dollar at seven and sixpence, and the like. The list of signers gives some notion of the families who remained in town when Howe drew near. Stansbury was of course one of them.

The

Notes to the Loyal Verses

The song itself, though set to a jingling nursery air, has its interest as showing how matters were carried on at the time. The Philadelphia market was almost bare of many articles of necessity, and of almost all of luxury, when the British came in. That of New York was in a better condition; and from it and from England cargoes were waiting to be discharged on the wharves at Philadelphia so soon as opportunity offered. Of course the profits were to be heavy; the more so, as being confined to a favoured few. On the 8th August, 1777, a writer from New York says: " For some time past the demand for goods of all sorts, and the
" high prices given for them, has made the fortunes of those who brought
" out cargoes with them. This lucrative traffic has been confined to a few
" favourites, chiefly Scotchmen. It was thought the British Prohibitory
" Act would have prevented the arrival, in America, of all British goods;
" but so far from it, that Act has thrown the *whole* trade into the hands of
" a few who make a monopoly of it. But the departure of the fleet and
" army, which has carried off 24,000 people, soldiers, sailors, and at-
" tendants, together with a proclamation issued out, prohibiting all inter-
" course with the Jerseys, has made trade very dull of late; however,
" many of those who came out lately, and have not got their cargoes sold,
" are reshipping their goods, to be ready to sail whenever intelligence
" arrives of Sir William Howe having made good his landing, where they
" intend to dispose of their goods to great advantage." The character of the supplies mentioned in the Song is amusing; and the arrival of the fleet of transports is spoken of as restoring to the docks of Philadelphia their former appearance of commercial prosperity. But there must have been a great scarcity of many of the ordinary staples of traffic before Howe appeared, as may be gathered from the fact of the importation of Irish beef: an article that had been theretofore prized for seastores in this country, but not for consumption on shore, where our own cattle were abundant. " For long voyages," says the testimony before the Embargo Committee in 1777, "Irish beef is preferred in America because it keeps
" better: there is not the smallest probability of its being preferred for
" the army."—*Almon's Remembrancer*, VIII: 207.

NOTE

Note 22, Page 22.

If the whigs of America had their troubles during the war, it must not be supposed that the tories slept upon a bed of roses. At Philadelphia even, where there were hundreds suspected of loyal proclivities, a tory was held by the whigs in 1774 as " the most despicable animal in the " creation. Spiders, toads, snakes, are their only proper emblem." So long as they continued passively loyal, they were subjected to affronts and indignities, but when hostilities became active, they felt the full weight of whig displeasure. It is but fair to add that on their side they were not remiss in seeking to injure their opponents. Every record of the time throws more or less light on this sad condition of affairs, the inevitable consequence of a civil war in any form or degree. Thus Marshall enters in his Diary, *January* 21st, 1777; " Deal of floating ice in the river, so " as to prevent the plunder of a number of Tories in the Jersies (part of " which, it's said to the amount of thirtyseven wagons, is arrived at Wil- " liam Cooper's ferry, &c.), from being brought over to this city." The tories in New Jersey were far more active than their Pennsylvania friends. In 1777, we find Alexander Hamilton urging Governor Livingston to visit with exemplary punishment all such, taken in arms or employed in enlisting men for the British service: and while Livingston hanged them for treason against the state when opportunity offered, Washington him- self saw the necessity of stringent measures against the most atrocious offenders, and thus wrote to Congress: "In this state, I have strong " assurance that the spirit of disaffection has risen to a great height; and " I shall not be disappointed if a large number of the inhabitants in some " of the counties should openly appear in arms, as soon as the enemy " begin their operations."

Note 23, Page 23.

Sir William Howe's bittereſt enemies never denied him the poſſeſſion of "thoſe military abilities which were demonſtrated in his manœuvres on Long Iſland and the Brandywine, and that undaunted courage which was ſo apparent in the action at Bunker's Hill." But his warmeſt friends muſt have perceived in his conduct of the American campaign, an alloy of ignoble traits that, under Cromwell or Napoleon, would have brought a commanding general to a very diſgraceful end.

In conſidering his career in America it muſt be borne in mind that great reſults were at firſt expected by his brother, Lord Howe, and himſelf, from the pacific powers with which, as Royal Commiſſioners, they were inveſted. It is very probable that Lord Howe, who was a purer character than Sir William, counted a great deal on the influence of Dr. Franklin and ſome other leaders in the American councils in favour of bringing about an accommodation. His interviews with Franklin on this ſubject, while the latter was yet in England, as related by the doctor himſelf, could not have inſpired him with very ſtrong faith in the ſucceſs of ſuch an undertaking: yet we muſt remember that each party may have looked at the event in a different light. It is certain that Lord Howe took every preliminary ſtep that was in his power to gain favour in the eyes of the Americans; among other evidences of which is the following letter (which I believe has not been publiſhed) from Mr. De Berdt, to James Kinſey, Eſq., of the New Jerſey Legiſlature.

London, May 5, 1776. *Sir:* My Brother in Law Joſeph Read Eſq. having particularly informed me the honor your Aſſembly has done me by chooſing me their Agent in November laſt, and how the obligation was encreaſed by the unanimity of the choice, give me leave Sir with the acknowledgment of the favor to attempt ſome proof of my attachment and regard to your Province and Country.

I would inform you that from public report there was the greateſt reaſon

reason to believe Lord Howe who is going out to America commander in chief of his Majesties Forces, &ca, &ca, had designs the most friendly & intentions of accommodating the unhappy differences without violence. I therefore did myself the honor to wait upon him and was so confirmed in my belief of what I had heard and so fully satisfied from his Lordship's conversation that he accepted his commission solely with a view to effect Peace, that I cannot help communicating to you a proposal which I am confident is the wish & desire of his Lordship & I think is your duty and interest. I do not write this merely as matter of opinion or recommend it as a prudent step only; but propose it from a full conviction of my judgement that it is reasonable—that it is right—and further I have assurances that it will be accepted and that no unreasonable concessions will be requested.

And tho' it is presumable that his Lordship's instructions are confined within the act of Parliament appointing Commissioners yet it is generally believed he has such dispensing powers that with a disposition to treat he is authorized to compromise & adjust.

What I mean is that immediately on Lord Howe's arrival a Parly or Conference be proposed between him and certain Deputies from among you to converse on the state of public affairs as Gentlemen & Friends.

The general report in England of his peacefull intentions confirmed from private conferences with some of your friends who have wrote to you on the subject begging that the matter may be taken into your most serious consideration and the particular respect which the people of America bear his Lordship and Family, added to his amiable character as an Officer and a Gentleman surely a parly may be brought about for some such reasons in which the dignity of his country will not be affected nor the honour of America called in question.

My real regard for America, my wish for peace and reconciliation, my faith in Lord Howe's personal assurances and my desire of giving early proof to your honorable House of Assembly that their appointment is fallen upon a Man who will ever make it the study of his Life to promote

the

the welfare and happiness of his constituents, these motives & these alone influence my Heart & actuate my Conduct.

However insuccessfull this humble attempt of mine may prove, I beg it may be remembered as a proof of my good wishes and intentions. I beg you will communicate this to the House, as *early* as possible and to accept my assurances of esteem & regard. I am your obliged and obedient hble servt. DENNIS DE BERDT.
Favored by Lord Howe.

With such credentials Lord Howe departed on his mission, in expectation, no doubt, of procuring an accommodation. In a contemporaneous manuscript notebook of George Chalmers, I find this memorandum: " C. Stewart says—that Lord H— having been assured by Dr. Franklin, " what would satisfy the Colonies, made it a point that he should be " empowered to grant these. He was empowered. He took privateers " on his voyage, but dismissed them, desiring them to say; Lord H— was " to make peace. *He told Arbuthnot, at Halifax, that peace would be* " *made within ten days after his arrival.*" Had he arrived in season, it is within the limits of possibility that he might have effected something, if we may draw any inferences from the anxiety displayed by the advocates for Independence in Congress to propagate the belief that there were no such Commissioners coming at all; and the attention that was given to the report by others who were not so warm in that cause. " We are waiting, " it is said," says Adams in April, 1776, " for commissioners; a messiah " that will never come. This story of commissioners is as arrant an illu- " sion as ever was hatched in the brain of an enthusiast, a politician, or a " maniac. I have laughed at it, scolded at it, grieved at it, and I don't " know but I may, in an unguarded moment, have rip'd at it. But it is " in vain to reason against such delusions. I was very sorry to see, in a " letter from the General [Washington] that he had been bubbled with " it; and still more, to see, in a letter from my sagacious friend, W. " [James Warren] at Plymouth, that he was taken in too." But Commissioners were coming, and it would be rendering slight justice to New England

England astuteness not to believe her delegates knew it. It is not at all improbable, in the opinion of some, that before the arrival of Sir William Howe at Sandy Hook on the 25th of June, and of Lord Howe at Staten Island on the 12th July, the prospect of encountering them as fellow-subjects and negotiators, instead of as foreigners and enemies, had been fully considered; and that the necessity of committing the colonies through their representatives, to an extent that would put an accommodation out of the question, had a great deal to do with the enactment on the 2nd July, of the resolution declaring " that these United Colonies are, and of " right ought to be, free and independent States." And accordingly, though the Howes waited for overtures from the whigs ere they commenced hostilities, and even directly invited just such a conference with members of congress as had been recommended by De Berdt (who probably was their mouthpiece in his letter), yet congress was now able to point to its record, and refuse to negotiate save on the footing of independency.

In the warfare that presently ensued, Sir William Howe frequently displayed good generalship: in fact it appears as though, when he himself felt that he *must* fight, his abilities were superior to those of any or all of his opponents. But he omitted to push his victories, and seemed determined to leave the Americans at least the nucleus of an army. After defeating the Americans on Long Island, a vigorous night-attack on their works would probably have demolished our army; instead of which, the next day saw them escaped to the main land. After the reduction of Fort Washington, when Greene retreated with the garrison of Fort Lee left it should share the same fate, Thomas Payne, who was with the troops, was of opinion that Howe committed another oversight, in not detaching a force from Staten Island through Amboy, whereby Greene's retreat into Pennsylvania might have been cut off, and the American magazines at Brunswick captured. " But," piously adds Payne, " if we believe the " power of hell to be limited, we must likewise believe that their agents " are under some providential controul." The criticisms of a civilian on

military

military affairs may not be worth much. Fortunately I have before me a series of manuscript memorandums by Sir Henry Clinton, on the events and conduct of the war, that may better test the value of Howe's services. Of the measure that led to the American victories of Trenton and Princeton, Sir Henry observes: "There were who thought (and were not silent) that a chain across Jersey might be dangerous. General Howe wrote to General Clinton thus a few days before the misfortune: 'I have been prevailed upon to run a chain across Jersey: the links are rather too far asunder.' * * * I am clear," Clinton continues, "it would have been better if Sir William Howe had not taken a chain across Jersey."

Of the maraudings in 1776-7 of the English in the Jerseys, Clinton says: "Unless we could refrain from plundering, we had no business to take up winter quarters in a district we wished to preserve loyal. The Hessians introduced it."

Of Howe's movement from New York against Philadelphia, he observes: "I owe it to truth to say there was not, I believe, a man in the army except Lord Cornwallis and General Grant who did not reprobate the move to the southward, and see the necessity of a coöperation with General Burgoyne."

Of Howe's suffering Washington to retreat, comparatively unpursued at the moment, from the field of Brandywine: "'Tis pity Sir William Howe could not have begun his march at nightfall, instead of eight o'clock in the morning."

Of Howe's crowning the campaign with the occupation of Philadelphia: "General Clinton told Lord George Germain, April 27th, and Sir William Howe repeatedly, after his return to America, his humble opinion that Philadelphia had better close than open the campaign, as it required an army to defend it."

Of the battle of Germantown and the check to the Americans occasioned by Musgrave's throwing himself with a few companies into Chew's House, Sir Henry makes a remark that, while it shews on what chances the fate of a battle may turn, does not at all support Howe's asseveration that

that his army was not furprifed: "Had Wafhington left a corps to ob-
"ferve this houfe, and proceeded, there is no faying what might have
"been the confequence."

But enough has been quoted to exhibit Sir William's deficiencies:
what their caufe was is another queftion. Tradition affigns a bafe motive
to him, in the affertion of a defire to increafe his fortune in procrafti-
nating the war, through underhand arranegments with thofe to whom
he affigned the privileges of trade, and others. He is faid to have been
the fecret partner of Coffin, a great trader under the royal flag. Harfh
as this fufpicion may found, it is confirmed by Horace Walpole's language
to Sir Horace Mann, in 1778: "General Howe is returned, richer in
"money than in laurels;" and by that of Adams, a year earlier:
"Thefe two Howes were very poor, and they have fpent the little for-
"tunes they had in bribery at elections; and having obtained feats in
"Parliament, and having fome reputation as brave men, they had nothing
"to do but to carry their votes and their valor to market, and, it is very
"true, they have fold them at a high price." During the period of his
command in America, there was fuch a corrupt mifmanagent of the fifcal
concerns of his army, as ftaggered even a Scottifh placehunter. "The
"peculation in every profitable branch of the fervice," wrote Wedder-
burn in 1777-8, "is reprefented to be enormous, and as ufual, it is attended
"with a fhocking neglect of every comfort to the troops. The hofpitals
"are pefthoufes, and the provifions ferved out are poifon: thofe that are
"to be bought, are fold at the higheft prices of a monopoly." It is eafy
to fee how, in this ftate of affairs, a venal commander might make his
own bargains with thofe with whom he would combine to defraud his
followers and his country. There is no pofitive evidence, however, that
Howe was guilty in this regard: the only proof we have is fuch as has
been recited and fuch loofe affertions as that contained in the goffip of the
times; a fpecimen of which may be found in the Verfes circulated in
Edinburgh in May, 1778, on occafion of equipping a new Scots regiment, and commencing, *How art thou fallen, poor John Bull!*—in which
reference is made to the Americans

Who

Who force thee from thy native right,
Becaufe thy Heroes will not fight:
(Perfidious men! who millions gain
By each protracted, flow campaign!)

Sir Nathaniel Wraxall fpeaks very plainly of the eftimate he put upon Sir William and his brother; they were "either lukewarm, or remifs, or "negligent, or incapable. Lord North's felection of thefe two com- "manders excited, at the time, juft condemnation. However brave, "able, or meritorious they might individually be efteemed as profeffional "men, their ardour in the caufe itfelf was doubted, and ftill more quef- "tionable was their attachment to the adminiftration. Never, perhaps, "in the hiftory of modern war, has an army or a fleet been more pro- "fufely fupplied with every requifite for brilliant and efficient fervice, "than were the troops and fhips fent out by Lord North's cabinet, in "1776, acrofs the Atlantic. But the efforts abroad did not correfpond "with the exertions made at home. The energy and activity of a "Wellington never animated that torpid mafs. Neither vigilance, enter- "prife, nor coöperation characterized the campaign of 1776 and 1777. "Diffipation, play, and relaxation of difcipline found their way into the "Britifh camp."

The fecret of the appointment may have been that North, knowing the profeffional abilities of the men; the efteem in which their relation- fhip to the Howe who was flain in America during the Seven Years' War entitled them to be held in that country; their political connexions with the Whigs in England; and perhaps, their kindred (on the wrong fide of the blanket, it is true—and indeed the fame was whifpered of the premier himfelf—) to the fovereign; was influenced by one or all of thefe confiderations to beftow on them the pofts in queftion. To carry this through, arrangements had to be made in regard to Sir Guy Carleton, the commander in Canada, who was Howe's fenior officer—an older foldier, and perhaps a better; at all events a more zealous and active one. Indeed, fuch was Howe's fluggifhnefs and love of pleafure in almoft every

form

form (see *Coll. Hift. Soc. Penn.*, 1, 120), that it is no great praise to say thus much of Carleton. Sir Walter Scott quotes from an old song in one of his letters

> General Howe is a gallant commander,
> There are others as gallant as he ;

and in Simcoe, a mere grenadier captain of the 40th, under Sir William's command, the stuff might have been found for a leader who, in Sir William's place, would have given a different turn to events. By the end of the winter of 1777-8, the ministry gave their general to understand that they were very ill content with what he had done, or rather with what he had left undone; and his pride or his prudence at once took umbrage. He already looked on Clinton as a rival; and had thus addressed Lord George Germain on this head: " I am led to hope that I may be re-
" lieved from this very painful service, wherein I have not the good
" fortune to enjoy the necessary support and confidence of my superiors,
" but which, I conclude, will be extended to Sir Henry Clinton, my pre-
" sumptive successor. By the return of the packet I humbly request I
" may have his Majesty's permission to resign." When the permission came, however, he discovered, if we are to believe that the American general Charles Lee rightly interpreted his sentiments, that he had all along been made use of as an instrument of ministerial wickedness and folly. Nothing can be more characteristic than the portrait Lee draws of Sir William: " He is naturally good humored, complaisant, but illite-
" rate and indolent to the last degree, unless as an executive soldier, in
" which capacity he is all fire and activity, brave and cool as Julius Cæsar.
" His understanding is, as I observed before, rather good than otherwise,
" but was totally confounded and stupified by the immensity of the task
" imposed upon him. He shut his eyes, fought his battles, drank his
" bottle, had his little ——, advised with his counsellors, received his
" orders from North and Germaine (one more absurd than the other),
" took Galloway's opinion, shut his eyes, fought again, and is now, I
" suppose,

"suppose, to be called to account for acting according to instructions." Lee thought that the conflict between Washington and Howe had resolved itself into a trial of the efficacy of their respective blunders. "It seemed to be a trial of skill, which party should outdo the other, and it is hard to say which played the deepest strokes; but it was a capital one of ours, which certainly gave the happy turn which affairs have taken. Upon my soul, it was time for Fortune to interpose, or we were inevitably lost." So far as his treatment of Americans was concerned, Howe's blunders were indeed capital. He incensed the whigs by his severities: he repelled the loyalists, by putting as little confidence in them as might be, and discouraging their organization and action in arms; and he wasted his time in futile efforts to open, through the medium of Sullivan, Lee, Willing, and other whigs, negotiations with Congress. He returned to England unpopular alike with the ministry and the nation, although followed by the applause of those whom he had commanded. Even at Nottingham, his own town, he was not acceptable to the inhabitants. Unlike his brother, who lived to do his country brilliant service and to add a fresher lustre to the maritime glory of England, Sir William was never again, so far as is generally known, invested with command. He appears to have succeeded to this brother's Irish Viscounty (the English peerage failing, for lack of a son to its possessor) and died in 1814.

Note 24, Page 24.

Though Discord, your generous zeal to oppose,
   Shall nourish sedition and hate,
Till your Friends feel the horrors of War with your Foes,
   Your success is ensur'd you by Fate.—*Author's Variation.*

Note 25, Page 25.

Hermes' Wand the fierce Snakes could no longer unite;
   Its Virtues they wholly defied:
The branch of the Olive did only affright,
   To see it at random applied.—*Author's Variation.*

Perhaps

Perhaps there may be an allusion here to the broken Snake, with the motto *Unite or Die*, so much in vogue at the time as a patriotic device.

Note 26, Page 29.

The efforts of the Philadelphians to obtain the commercial restoration of their colonial paper currency have been dwelt upon in a previous note. This poem commemorates the failure of their endeavours.

Note 27, Page 29.

While the style of Dr. Smith's Oration may have recommended it to the loyal bard, it probably lost nothing, in his estimation, by the circumstance of its author losing grace in the eyes of Congress. "The oration "was an insolent performance," says Mr. Adams. " A motion was "made to thank the Orator, and ask a copy, but opposed with great spirit "and vivacity from every part of the room, and at last withdrawn, lest "it should be rejected, as it certainly would have been, with indignation. "The Orator then printed it himself, after leaving out or altering some "offensive passages. This is one of the most irregular and extravagant "characters of the age. I never heard one single person speak well of "anything about him but his abilities, which are generally allowed to be "good. The appointment of him to make the oration was a great over-"sight and mistake." The objection urged in Congress to the motion was that the Orator had declared them to be still anxious for a dependency upon Great Britain. The motion was sustained, though fruitlessly, by William Livingston, Duane, Thomas Willing, James Wilson, &c.

Note 28, Page 30.

—Nor lost or dead or founder'd Horse:
I would to Heaven it were no worse.
But fain I must your Patience ask
While I perform the mournful task;
—So mournful, I could weep, *my honey*—
Alas! the Death of Paper Money.—*Author's Variation.*

Whether Howe or Mongomery be aimed at in the firſt part of the paragraph referred to by this note, the reader may decide. Perhaps the poet, in no very amiable mood at the time, when Howe's conduct had reduced to worthleſſneſs the moneybags of many of the citizens, may have purpoſely dealt in an ambiguous expreſſion. As to the *Want of Bread* which threatened him and his friends, left thus in the lurch without available funds, the prices that proviſions bore in Philadelphia at that period would ſeem to warrant his alarm. Before the Americans withdrew, the better claſſes had been forced in great meaſure to relinquiſh the uſe ſo Weſt India goods. " Milk has become the breakfaſt of many of the " wealthieſt and genteeleſt families here." Loaf ſugar ſold then at four dollars a pound; brown ſugar of the pooreſt quality at a dollar; and New England rum at forty ſhillings a gallon. After the royal army entered the city, and before the arrival of the fleet, beef was at three and nine pence (half a dollar) and butter at ſeven and ſix pence (one dollar) the pound; and this in ſpecie. And before the winter was over, even theſe difficult times were made more arduous to be endured. In February, 1778, flour commanded three guineas the hundred weight, and all other proviſions were at a proportional rate. Congreſs had made it a capital felony for any inhabitant of Pennſylvania or New Jerſey to ſupply proviſions to Philadelphia, and the American patrolling parties made it an eſpecial point to cut off all ſuch perſons as, tempted by the prices their commodities brought in that market, would ſeek to evade or defy the decree. As the troops were well furniſhed with garriſon rations, this prohibition fell moſt ſeverely on the citizens of the town; and its rigour forced a parliamentary admiſſion of its injuſtice from Marſhal Conway, one of the ſteadieſt opponents of the Engliſh miniſtry. He ſtated correctly the military principle " that when the hope of ſubduing an enemy " by ſtarving made the penalty of ſupplying them with proviſions *death*, " then thoſe who were the treſpaſſers did it at their peril, and the general " who publiſhed the order was juſtified: but in no other caſe." In theſe ſtraits, the leading Quaker gentry of Philadelphia were, it is ſaid, compelled

pelled to make applications to Dr. Fothergill and others of their perfuafion at London, for relief, to be repaid at the end of the troubles.

Note 29, Page 30.

With grief the Mufe proceeds and tells.—*Author's Variation.*

Note 30, Page 35.

On the 29th of January, 1778, Sir James Wallace of the *Experiment* (a fourth-rater of fifty guns), brought as a prize into New York the Lady Margaret, a Dutch veffel of 600 tons, commanded by Captain De Ruyter and bound from Cadiz to Carolina on account of Congrefs. Her cargo chiefly confifted in 5000 pounds of Jefuit's Bark; wine; falt; brandy; cordage; linens; tea; medicines; and mercer's ware: articles of the firft neceffity to our army. The prize was a rich one; and there was an additional fatiffaction to the royalifts in its detection while engaged in the trade with the Americans that it was well known France and Holland were covertly carrying on.

As for Wallace himfelf, he feems to have been a brutal fort of a feadog; fomething after the now happily obfolete ftyle of Sir Hawfer Trunnion. "His character upon the coaft was that of being brutal and info-"lent beyond his peers," fays one of his acquaintance: and his behaviour on fhore was that of a man who would fwear at a lady and bully a clergyman or a Quaker. On one occafion, at a fupper table in Philadelphia, he purfued a Quaker with a deal of vulgar raillery and farcafm, till the latter was tempted to refort, if not to the weapon of the carnal Adam, at leaft to that of the reprefentatives of our mother Eve. "Captain," faid the "friend, thou haft made very free with me, and afked me a great many "queftions, which I have endeavoured to anfwer to thy fatiffaction: wilt "thou now permit me to afk thee one in my turn?" "Oh, by all means," anfwered Sir James; "any thing that you pleafe, friend—what is it? "Why, then, I wifh to be informed what makes thee drink fo often?
"Art

"Art thou really dry, every time thou carrieſt the liquor to thy mouth?" "What," ſcreamed Wallace in a guſt of rage—"what! do you think I am a hog, only to drink when I am dry!" The Quaker retreated under a valley of oaths, ſatiſfied no doubt with the homethruſt he had inflicted. Wallace was however a good ſailor; and though he and the Experiment were taken by D'Eſtaing's fleet in September, 1779, he was ſoon at ſea again. Indeed the Experiment itſelf is reported as being at Gibraltar in June, 1780, and in July Wallace himſelf, in command of the Nonſuch, juſt after completing the deſtruction of the *Legere*, a French frigate, was ſo lucky as to fall in with and capture *La Belle Poule*, renowned in naval ſong for her encounter with the "ſaucy Arethuſa." In 1783 he made a ſenſation in London by proſecuting to conviction Mr. Bourne, of the Marines, for an aſſault, to the unqualified diſguſt of the corps: which paſſed a reſolve that no gentleman bearing his majeſty's commiſſion ought to go out with a man who, having been publicly caned, &c., thought fit to ſeek for his redreſs in a Court of Juſtice.

Note 31, Page 35.

You Tories compare theſe poor devils to Mites, who always deſtroy the ſubſtance that gives them life and ſupport.—*Author's Note*.

Note 32, Page 35.

The Experiment man of war commanded by Sir James.—*Author's Note*.

Note 33, Page 35.

Brandy won't ſave them—"as the ſaying is." *⁎* The Ship's Cargo conſiſted of the above mentioned articles.—*Author's Note*.

Note 34, Page 36.

Such affociations as the Church-and-King club were not of unufual occurrence with the loyalifts. They were generally defigned to bring together at the dinner table a party of men whofe political fentiments were in unifon. In this inftance, the members were probably Philadelphians, who had followed the royal ftandard to New York: the phrafe, *'tis all the fame in Dutch*, being a local expreffion arifing from the numbers of German fettlers in Pennfylvania. To the firft two lines of the burthen the author gives a variation:

> Let old Diogenes fettle the nation;
> He ne'er had a drop of good wine in his tub.

Note 35, Page 36.

The allufion to the Howes in this verfe is fufficiently clear. The capture of Burgoyne's army at Saratoga, and his dinner with General Gates, is alfo referred to.

Note 36, Page 36.

It was frequently declared, at this period, by the advocates of England, that Congrefs had given fecretly fome fort of a lien upon part of the American territories to France, as a fecurity for the affiftance afforded us by that power. Of courfe there was no truth in the report. The exultations of the Americans, and of Congrefs in particular, was however (and naturally fo) very great, at the profpect of the refults to flow from fuch a connexion as the confederation had now formed. The firft anniverfary of the day on which the Treaty was figned was celebrated by a banquet given by Congrefs to the French Minifter; at which the King and Queen of France, the King of Spain, and all the Princes of the Houfe of Bourbon, were formally toafted, under falvos of artillery. On the

the 8th of May, 1778, Congrefs had iffued an addrefs to the people, in which the certainty of victory over England was proclaimed, and a warm picture given of the profperity which would then attend the deftinies of the United States.

Note 37, Page 39.

Nothing more vigourous than *The Town Meeting* is to be found among all the loyal fatires produced during the revolutionary war; nor was its popularity furpaffed by that of any other of its clafs. That it hit the whigs feverely, and that its perfonalities were fhrewdly aimed, is evident to any one familiar with the hiftory of the times: and Stanfbury's familiarity with the people and politics of Philadelphia enabled him to eafily bring into fucceffful ridicule many of thofe fubordinate characters of the drama—*Glaucumque, Medontaque, Therfilochumque*—who rarely figure in ifolated pofitions on the pages of hiftory. The refult has been ftated in an earlier Note; the refentment of this clafs fubfifted in ftrength fufficient to prevent his return to the city after the Peace, while that of more important characters had long faded away. Men who are unaccuftomed to public admiration are generally unforgiving of public cenfure, or farcafm.

Unlike the majority of the author's productions that have appeared in this volume, *The Town Meeting* is not printed from his original manufcript. But as it was firft publifhed under his own infpection, that text has been taken as a ftandard for comparifon with a number of contemporaneous manufcript copies in various hands. One of thefe, formerly among the papers of the late Edward Duffield of Moreland, was printed feveral years fince, in an edition of ten copies, by the late Edward D. Ingraham; viz: The Town Meeting: A Tory Squib. From the Copy found among the Papers of the late Edward Duffield, Efquire, of Moreland. Le bon vieux temps. Philadelphia, 1837. 8 vo. pp. 8.

Another, though a flightly incorrect verfion is given in Watfon's Annals of Philadelphia, II; 204.

To properly comprehend the verfes, the condition of affairs exifting in the

the city at the period must be present to the reader. The new constitution of Pennsylvania, adopted in 1776, was bitterly opposed by the moderate whigs, and also by almost every one who was not an active whig. It was supported in great measure by what John Adams called " the democratic " party." That it was first conceived or put forward to gratify the desires of the wealthier and graver classes of the population is improbable. There were whispers that it was the fruit of the promptings of certain New England delegates in Congress, who were dissatisfied with any line likely to be pursued by an Assembly chosen exclusively by electors with a freehold qualification; and who therefore devised these means of procuring an alteration in the character of the provincial legislature. If there was any truth in this suggestion, John Adams could not have been involved in the business, for he had no good opinion of the new frame of government. His colleague Samuel Adams, however, intrigued so keenly to saddle it on a community of which he was not a citizen, as to provoke, according to Gordon, some persons " to drop distant hints of an assassination." Once in operation, its power was wielded exclusively by the people that had procured its adoption; and if some, who at first decried its suitability to the wants and the rights of the inhabitants, afterwards became its expounders, it was because there was no other means of obtaining civil authority in the State than by the aid of the new party.

In the mean time, the financial condition of the country was producing an effect on the minds of men. Up to 1779, there had been emitted, by Congress, about sixty millions of dollars in paper money, which was then in circulation and unredeemed. There was also due by the United States, for moneys borrowed, about forty millions more. The terms of the articles of confederation gave Congress no sufficient power to raise the means of discharging these debts: indeed, all the states, though represented in that body, had not as yet consented to the Confederation. At the period in question, the Continental Treasury had received in all but about three millions of dollars for taxes. It is therefore very plain that the Continental Paper Money could have had no other commercial value than what

arose

arose from the common consent to give and take it in some proportion or other to its nominal value. Tender laws, which compelled creditors to receive it, or have their debts cancelled by refusal, served only to injure a certain number of mortgagees or bondholders; they could not endow the paper money with vitality. Nothing of course could do this but a reasonable ground of belief in its eventual redemption by the United States; and the practical comment upon the justice of such a belief may be seen in the bushels of bills that cumbered, within the recollection of the present generation, more than one old garret. Accordingly, the value of the notes issued by Congress was daily decreasing through all the war: so that while in 1780 three hundred pounds in this currency would buy a dog, and three thousand an ox and a half and a few eggs; in 1781, seven hundred pounds in paper represented but ten in specie; and a mob is said to have paraded through the streets of Philadelphia with colors flying and cockades of paper dollars in their hats, escorting a dog which had been tarred and then stuck over, not with feathers, but with congressional paper money. In the next year this currency found its real value, at which it has remained ever since.

The compulsory laws, which forced creditors to receive this money, could have produced no good effect on the morals of the community. Watson observes that one of the worst uses to which it was put " was to " present it as 'a legal tender,' to pay with almost no value what had been " before purchased for a *bona fide* valuable confideration. Many base men " so acquired their property: especially when 'to cheat a tory' was deemed " fair prize with several. Houses still stand in Philadelphia, which, could " their walls speak out, would tell of strangely inconsiderable values re- " ceived for them by the sellers. The large double house, for instance, " at the north-west corner of Second and Pine streets, was once purchased, " it was said, with the money received for one hogshead of rum. The " lot in Front, below Pine, whereon four or five large houses stood, called " Barclay's Row, was sold for £60 only of real value." When however the continued depreciation of the bills had reached a point that rendered

their

their own poſſeſſions unſafe, the whigs generally began to be uneaſy. Day by day its value decreaſed with the increaſe of its amount. A man might ſell a barrel of flour for a hundred pounds today, and tomorrow it would coſt him, to repurchaſe it, a hundred and twenty. Naturally, the prices of all ſorts of commodities were regulated by the value of the money with which they were to be bought. The ſmall dealers, who to a great extent ſold their own produce, were juſt as careful to follow the ſcale of depreciation as the extenſive merchant whoſe warehouſes were filled with goods. But as the latter very often ſought to obtain the control of the market by ſecuring, for the time being, the command of the ſupply, he was conſtantly liable to fall within the category of foreſtallers and monopoliſts. To prevent, therefore, the depreciation of the money, the authorities of the day contemplated the limitation of prices; while the government of Pennſylvania, in January, 1779, declared its intention of enforcing the heavieſt penalties againſt foreſtallers. Unfortunately, however, there would appear to have been ſuch a ſpice of partizan politics infuſed into the conſideration of this branch of the queſtion as to give room to ſuppoſe at the time that private as well as public motives would enter into the enforcement of theſe penalties. Robert Morris was then held in great diſlike by the party in the commonwealth that he was oppoſed to; and he was alſo the principal holder of flour among the merchants. He had, at this period, a contract for procuring large quantities of that article for the French fleet. In furtherance of their objects, a town meeting was held at Philadelphia on the 25th of May, 1779. The popular excitement, already ſufficiently great, was ſtimulated to fever heat by a parade of the militia on the day previous, as narrated by the poet in Canto Firſt: the proceedings of the meeting itſelf are in a meaſure told in Canto Second. But as it may not be amiſs to give a connected account of the concluſion as well as of the beginning of this buſineſs, this Note will be carried to a greater length. I have before me a broadſide account of the occaſion, evidently publiſhed by authority of the officers of the day for the information of the public. The Chairman, General Roberdeau, after a ſpeech

in

in which the evils of forestalling were dwelt upon; the orator's conviction declared that a combination had been formed for raising the prices of goods and provisions; the necessity of such combinations being put down by the people asserted; and the fact expatiated on, that during the past six months prices had risen week by week: then introduced a series of resolutions that had been prepared beforehand by a committee of citizens. These pointed out Robert Morris by name as the ostensible actor in bringing about the recent rise of prices, and ordered that a committee should investigate his conduct, and that he should answer in writing the interrogatories to be put to him: that the prices of West India goods, tea, flour, &c., should instantly be reduced to the rates of May 1st; that offenders against these resolutions should be noticed by the committee; that the conduct of suspected public officers under Congress be examined into by another committee; that all persons "inimical to the interest and " independence of the United States" should be expelled from the community, &c. These resolutions were, after some debate, agreed to. On the next day (May 26th), General Joseph Reed, Mr. Bayard, and some others, presented a memorial to Congress on the same subjects as had occasioned the meeting: it was referred to a committee of which John Dickinson was chairman; and an answer presently appeared that was not at all satisfactory to those who presented the memorial. On the 26th of May, the Committee appointed at the Town Meeting on the 25th, published a tariff of prices; at which rates only were people to be permitted to buy and sell. In June, another and a yet lower tariff was adopted, and the Committee made its power felt by several of the chief merchants, whose conduct had not tallied with the will of the people. Morris in especial was the subject of indignation. His own statement of his position, and of the disturbances to which his business had been subjected, will be found in the local newspapers of the day. On the 26th July, the Committee, through William Bradford, Esq., its chairman, published an Address, in which the justice and expediency of their conduct was maintained, and the fact declared that the result of the Town Meeting in May had been

been to put a stop to the depreciation of paper money. The remonstrance of eighty merchants who avowed, in the opening of their representation, that since the days of the Stamp Act they had been steady and decided whigs, was published about the same time. It was more reasonable than the Address of the Committee, but it produced less effect. It was in vain that they urged that they had to contend, in making their purchases, with the same depreciation that their customers were aggrieved by: that a vessel, for instance, such as formerly could be bought for £600 or £700, now cost upwards of £40,000. A considerable portion of the inhabitants were resolute to sustain the Committee, and would not be convinced by anything that could be said by men whom party rage confounded with concealed Tories. In the end of June, a militia company of artillery declared its desire to take up arms against their fellow-citizens in support of the decrees of the Town Meeting and the Committee; and through the summer, the illwill and excitement was constantly on the increase. Morris, McClenachan, and other prominent characters were openly menaced, and placards were posted, on the morning of October 4th, threatening the breaking open of their stores. A meeting of the Militia was called for that morning, the object of which was undoubtedly violence; and the mob, including a number of armed militia-men, took up their line of march through the city. It is not known now what particular end they had in view: but probably their intent was to act, as circumstances might suggest, against all obnoxious persons. They had already seized two such individuals, when they arrived at the dwelling of James Wilson, at the corner of Walnut and Third Streets. Wilson was a whig, and a Signer of the Declaration of Independence; but he was of the same political creed as Robert Morris; and was additionally odious to the government party by reason of his services as a lawyer, to a number of persons not long before indicted for High Treason. He was therefore among those threatened with popular vengeance; and some thirty or forty of his friends had assembled at his house to defend him. It would seem that this party comprised several who were marked by the mob. Very happily, however,

ever, General Mifflin was one of the number, who was a warm political enemy of General Reed, the head of the executive of the ſtate. Mifflin had very ſagaciouſly adviſed that information of the approaching aſſault ſhould be ſent to General Reed, and his counſel had been carried into effect. The houſe being preſently attacked, and life loſt upon either ſide, Mifflin threw open a window, and attempted to addreſs the mob. A man immediately diſcharged his piece at him, the ball ſtriking the window-faſh cloſe by his body; on which the General returned the fire with both his piſtols. A byſtander relates that he queſtioned the aſſailant if he knew whoſe life he had aimed at: "he replied 'he ſuppoſed ſome damned " Tory,' and when I informed him that it was General Mifflin, he ex- " preſſed his ſurpriſe and regret." The mob, however, was repulſed, and for the moment retired. It preſently returned with cannon; and a party of men armed with ſledge-hammers and iron bars ſoon made a breach in the houſe. The arrival of General Reed with a couple of Baylor's dragoons, cauſed the aſſailants to pauſe; and very ſoon after a few of the Firſt City Troop charging into the crowd, it was completely diſperſed. The defenders of the houſe then ſallied out, and aided in the ſeizure of priſoners.

It is ſtated by Watſon that, in anticipation of the affray, the Troop (which was then as now compoſed of the gentry of the neighborhood) had prepared on this day to be ready for ſervice at a moment's warning. The deceitful calm that prevailed during the morning had induced the members to retire for dinner to their reſpective homes, and it was only nine of their number who were got together in time to act. Charging ſuddenly on the mob, ignorance of their real ſtrength aided the panic of their adverſaries; and the cry of "*the horſe, the horſe!*" was a ſignal for general flight. The party incurred great odium by this feat, and Major Lenox " was particularly marked out for deſtruction." His houſe at Germantown was ſubſequently ſurrounded in the night-time, and nothing but the opportune arrival of the Troop diſperſed his enemies. In alluſion to his having thrown aſide his long coat, to avoid being dragged from his horſe

on

on the 4th of October, and thus riding into action in his shirt-sleeves, he was for years after accosted as "brother butcher" in the market-place. Watson also gives the names of some of the defenders of the house: "Messrs. Wilson, Morris, Burd, George and Daniel Clymer, John T. "Mifflin, Allen McLane, Sharpe Delaney, George Campbell, Paul Beck, "Thomas Laurence, Andrew Robinson, John Potts, Samuel C. Morris, "Captain Campbell, and Generals Mifflin, Nichols, and Thompson. "They were provided with arms, but their stock of ammunition was "very small. While the mob was marching down, General Nichols and "Daniel Clymer proceeded hastily to the Arsenal at Carpenter's Hall, and "filled their pockets with cartridges: this constituted their sole supply. "* * * Allen McLane and Colonel Grayson got into the house after the "fray began. The mob called themselves *Constitutionalists*. Benezet's "fire in the entry from the cellar passage was very effective." John Schaffer, and Colonel Chambers of Lancaster, were also in the house. Captain Campbell was killed: he had served in Hazen's Continental Regiment and had lost an arm. Indeed most of the defenders seem to have been connected with the Continental Army, while their opponents were chiefly of the Militia. Such of the latter as had been arrested after their repulse, were sent to gaol. On the next day, the Militia Officers assembled, and there were apprehensions that they would enforce the release of their comrades. The matter ended by the prisoners being discharged on bail; and the party in the house were also compelled to enter into recognizances. No other legal proceedings were taken by the government of the State, save an act of general pardon to all concerned in the affair, whereby both sides escaped without trial and without punishment.

This tragic conclusion terminated the scene which had occupied the public stage since the 25th of May; and the opposite parties amongst the whigs were thenceforth more tranquil in their hostility. It is noticeable, however, that the flame kindled during 1779 never entirely burned out so long as some of those who shared in the excitement survived. It was the

belief

belief of more than one of his enemies that General Reed was implicated in the defign of the riot: but the charge is not fupported. Watfon remarks that General Arnold came to reprefs the mob, but he was fo unpopular that they ftoned him. Arnold was Reed's open enemy. He arrived with his weapons at Wilfon's houfe juft after the riot was quelled, and turning to the byftanders, obferved: " Your Prefident has raifed a " mob, and now he cannot quell it." Reed was ill in bed when the riot occurred; and feveral years after, in reference to the remark that he had gone to quell it at the rifk of his life, I find this ftatement in the manufcript of a Philadelphian who certainly bore him no good will: " That is true: " for, as he had raifed the mob, it was infifted he fhould go out and " and quiet them, and his life was threatened if he did not."

The feventeenth and eighteenth Stanzas of the Second Canto of *The Town Meeting* are quoted in the Life and Correfpondence of Prefident Reed, volume 2nd, page 149: which fhows that Stanfbury's fatiric fhafts did not, in every inftance, penetrate very deeply.

For other particulars of this crifis in the revolutionary hiftory of Pennfylvania, which for a moment fo nearly threatened the inauguration of fcenes fuch as thofe that a few years later tranfpired in France, fee *Reed's Reed*, II; c. 6: *Biog. Signers*, VI; 150. The local newfpapers of the day appear to have refrained from the flighteft allufion to the *emeute*.

Note 38, Page 39.

Watfon makes this ftanza refer to General Reed, but he is in error, it would feem. " John Bayard, for a time Speaker of the Pennfylvania " Affembly, and a Major in the regiment of which Mr. Roberdeau was " Colonel and Mr. Reed Lieutenant-Colonel " is believed to be the perfon alluded to. As early as 1774, Mr. Bayard was an active whig in the politics of High Street Ward, Philadelphia. Early in 1776 he and Roberdeau fitted out a privateer which foon captured a valuable prize. In 1785 he was a member of Congrefs, and died in 1807. His nephew, James A. Bayard, was one of the American negotiators at Ghent, and his

his great-nephews are also diftinguifhed in the public fervice. *To fave one's bacon* is an Americanifm, then as now in vogue: "A fuperior "fquadron of our allies may come upon the coaft in time to fave our "bacon; there I confefs I reft my almoft only hope."—*Gates to Reed,* 10th May, 1780.

NOTE 39, Page 40.

Blair M'Clenachan was a leading merchant in Philadelphia, and an active whig. A New York letter of April 19th, 1780, fays: "Yefter- "day arrived in our harbour the brigantine *Macaroni*, commanded by " —— Patterfon, belonging to Mr. Blair M'Lanachan, of Philadelphia. "She mounts 14 guns, is a perfect beauty, and was taken by his Majefty's "fhip Delight, Captain Inglis." In June of the fame year, he fubfcribed £10,000 to the eftablifhment of the Bank of Pennfylvania, of which he was chofen Infpector with Robert Morris, and three more. Morris fubfcribed a like fum. The object of this inftitution was to facilitate the obtaining fupplies for the army. Of other characters referred to in *The Town Meeting*, it may be added here that Jofeph Reed fubfcribed £2000; Thomas M'Kean, John Mitchell, and Benjamin Rufh, £2000 each; and Michael Hillegas, £4000: by which it appears that the friends and foes of 1779 were willing to unite for the good of the country in 1780. In 1782, it has been faid that he loft heavily, by engaging in a fort of licenfed gambling, cuftomary in former times. An account was publifhed, in Rivington's (New York) Gazette, of Rodney's victory over the Count de Graffe, and of the capture of the *Ville de Paris*, the French Admiral's flag-fhip. Rivington's paper was of fo little credit with the whigs, that none of them believed the ftory: and they were confirmed in their opinions by the arrival of an American privateer whofe people had witneffed the commencement only of the engagement; but whofe account of what they faw varied widely from Rivington's ftatement. In addition, the *Ville de Paris* was fo large and powerful a fhip that the officers of a French veffel, captured by the Englifh fome time after, being informed

of

of the refult of the engagement, were exceedingly downcaſt until they were told of the flagſhip's misfortune: on which their fpirits immediately revived:—" it was all a miſtake, a delufion," they cried;—" the *Ville de Paris* could not poffibly be taken." But William Bingham, Efq., who had means of obtaining very good intelligence from the Weſt Indies, had probably received fecret but authentic tidings: at leaſt it was fo reported at Philadelphia foon after. He therefore commenced to open policies on the fafety of the *Ville de Paris* with all who would underwrite her. Thefe were chiefly the warm and wealthy whigs, and M'Clenachan is faid to have been of the number. Bingham and his friends paid at firſt 10 *per cent* premium, and from that up to 25 and 30 *per cent*. Some four or five hundred thoufand dollars were thus underwritten. The one fide was encouraged in its miſtake by a letter received by the French Miniſter, written from Martinico after the battle, that gave caufe to believe the *Ville de Paris* had not been taken; while the other relied on its own intelligence, whatever that might have been. After the war, M'Clenachan was fued in England by one *Brag* for damages caufed by him while acting under public authority from the Americans. This proceeding, however unjuſt in itfelf, was balanced by the New York Statute of 17th March, 1783, prefcribing fimilar meafures againſt the other fide. He finally failed in bufinefs, and was impriſoned for debt. He was a warm anti-federaliſt: his propofition at a public meeting during Waſhington's adminiſtration, 'to kick Jay's Treaty to hell' excited much merriment at the time. He feems to have been a warmhearted, enthufiaſtic man, and a liberal friend to the American caufe during the war.

Note 40, Page 40.

Art. IV. " That all power being originally inherent in, and confequently derived from, the people; therefore all officers of government, whether legiſlative or executive, are their truſtees and fervants, and at all times accountable to them."—*Pennfylvania Conſtitution of* 1776: *Chap. i.*

NOTE 41, Page 40.

Robert Morris, Benedict Arnold, and (according to a manuscript note) William Wistar, are here referred to. The first was as distinguished for his abilities as a financier, as the second for his reckless and persevering courage as a soldier. This was while he was stationed at Philadelphia, and before his treason. Wistar was perhaps a citizen of Germantown.

NOTE 42, Page 40.

"Benjamin Paschall, Esquire; Justice of the Peace, and Shoemaker."
—*Author's Note.*

NOTE 43, Page 40.

The green sprig of foliage sometimes worn in the hat by the Americans, in lieu of a cockade.

NOTE 44, Page 41.

If the barber who shaved John Adams, and who figures so amusingly in Adams's letters to his wife of 23rd April, 1776, and 28th March, and 23rd April, 1777, was a fair type of their politics, the barbers of Philadelphia must have been staunch whigs. Adams describes him as a dapper little fellow, with an untiring tongue; a sergeant in one of the militia battalions; and troubled with remorse at missing his chance of fortune in the *Rattlesnake* privateer, which with the *Sturdy Beggar*, had taken eleven fine prizes. "Confound the ill luck, Sir; I was going to sea my-
" self on board the *Rattlesnake*, and my wife fell a yelping. These wives
" are queer things. I told her I wondered she had no more ambition.
" 'Now,' says I, 'when you walk the streets and any body asks who that
" is? The answer is *Burne the barber's wife*. Should you not be better
" pleased to hear it said, *That is Captain Burne's lady*, the Captain of
" marines on board the *Rattlesnake?*' 'O,' says she, 'I would rather
" be

"called Burne the barber's wife, than Captain Burne's widow. I don't
"desire to live better than you maintain me, my dear.' So it is, Sir, by
"this sweet, honey language, I am choused out of my prizes, and must
"go on with my soap and razors and pincers and combs. I wish she
"had my ambition."

Note 45, Page 41.

A manuscript note supplies here the name of a person "whipp'd at
"Annapolis: now a Committee-man."

Note 46, Page 41.

"Dr. Fallon, chairman of one of the Committees."—*Manuscript Note*.

Note 47, Page 41.

One manuscript of *The Town Meeting* has *Porter Mich.* and adds this note to the whole line: "The one a Porter, the other a Fisherman; now "Captains in the Army." Watson also reads Mich.; and the version printed from the Duffield copy says *Pewterer* Will. I prefer to follow the text in Rivington. *Mich.* might possibly refer to Michael Hillegas, a whig of considerable local influence; but the description of his antecedents will not apply. *Will* may signify Colonel Will, afterwards Sheriff of Philadelphia County.

Note 48, Page 41.

"John Mitchell, famous for eating Shad-roe," says a note in the Duffield impression. He is referred to in the third Stanzas of this Canto. In 1777, Colonel Mitchell was Adjutant-General of Pennsylvania. The Marquis de Chastellux in a sketch of one of the City Assembly Balls at Philadelphia in the winter of 1780-1 (where the airs danced to, by the way, went by the names of *Burgoyne's Defeat, The Success of the Campaign, Clinton's Retreat,* &c.) says: "The Managers are generally chosen
"from

"from amongſt the moſt diſtinguiſhed officers of the Army; this import-
"ant place is at preſent held by Colonel *Wilkinſon*, who is alſo a clothier-
"general of the Army. Colonel *Mitchell*, a little fat, ſquat man, fifty
"years old, a great judge of horſes, and who was lately Contractor for
"carriages, both for the American and the French Armies, was formerly
"the Manager; but when I ſaw him, he had deſcended from the magiſ-
"tracy, and danced like a private citizen. He is ſaid to have exerciſed
"his office with great ſeverity, and it is told of him, that a young lady
"who was figuring in a Country Dance, having forgot her turn by con-
"verſing with a friend, he came up to her, and called out aloud, *give over,*
"*Miſs, take care what you are about: Do you think you came here for*
"*your pleaſure?*"

Note 49, Page 41.

Thomas M'Kean; a Member of the Congreſs of 1765, a Signer of the Declaration; and the only man who was conſtantly a Member of Congreſs from 1774 to 1783. He was Preſident of Congreſs in 1781; Chief-Juſtice; and Governor of Pennſylvania. He may have dreſſed in black, as deſcribed by the poet, in private life: but on the bench he was diſtinguiſhed by his immenſe cocked-hat and ſcarlet gown. He died in 1817, in his 84th year.

Note 50, Page 41.

Continental Paper Money.

Note 51, Page 42.

Timothy Matlack: in 1780 a Member of Congreſs from Pennſylvania.

Note 52, Page 42.

Colonel John Bull of Philadelphia county; afterwards of Montgomery county. In 1772, he was a Juſtice of the Peace; in 1777, he was Colonel of the Firſt Regiment of Pennſylvania Levies; and a Member of Aſſembly from Philadelphia County. He commanded at Billingſport; and was Adjutant General of the Militia.

Note 53, Page 42.

"Daniel Roberdeau, a lumber merchant and militia general."—*Manuſcript Note.* A Member of Congreſs with Robert Morris from Pennſylvania in 1777; and that body meeting at York, where accommodations were ſcanty, he opened his houſe to Gerry, and Samuel and John Adams, delegates from Maſſachuſetts. Though of French extraction, he was a great public favourite at Philadelphia, where he had long dwelt. The following Warrant, iſſued (if genuine) when the Whigs there were preparing to fly before the enemy, is not printed in the Archives.—" In " *Council of Safety*, Philadelphia, Dec. 9, 1776. You are hereby au- " thorized and required to impreſs either *James Pemberton's, John Pem-* " *berton's, Samuel Emlen's*, jun., or *John Reynolds'* cloſe carriage and " horſes, for to remove General Roberdeau. By Order of Council, " *David Rittenhouſe, V. Preſident.* To John Bray, or any other Con- " ſtable." Theſe coach owners were probably not very zealous whigs. . Roberdeau's education muſt have been good. In 1777, we find him writing to ſeveral of the State Authorities, aſking that copies of Virgil and of Ovid ſhould be ſent him; which might have occaſioned the ſatiriſt, who reflected that the legiſlature of 1778 could not all write their own names, to repeat how often it happened that " the moſt capricious poet, " honeſt Ovid, was among the Goths." In January, 1795, Adams writes: " The public prints announce the death of my old, eſteemed friend, " General Roberdeau, whoſe virtues in heart-ſearching times endeared
" him

"him to Philadelphia and to his country. His friendly attention to me when Congress held their sessions at Yorktown I can never forget," &c. He is buried at Alexandria.

Note 54, Page 42.

Goshen is not remote from New York; which city, being the British headquarters, is here signified. The expulsion of the wives and children of Tories was not, in so many words, included in the Resolutions of the Town Meeting of May 25th: but the presence in the city of the wives of "British Emissaries" was presented as "a grievance of a very dangerous nature" by the Grand Jury, in July, 1779: and in June, 1780, the Executive Council of the State ordered that the wives and children of all persons who had joined the Enemy, if found within the State after the lapse of ten days from the date of that Decree, should be proceeded against as public enemies.

Note 55, Page 43.

" The mob are not easily pleas'd. While General Roberdeau was speaking from the chair, those behind him hiss'd and silenc'd him, because he turn'd his face from them."—*Author's Note.*

Note 56, Page 43.

Dr. James Hutchinson: born 1752; died of yellow fever, 1793. He was by birth a Quaker. See his biography in *Reed's Reed*, II; 127; and a free notice of his character in *Littell's Graydon*, 91. John Adams too must have disliked him excessively, when he repeated what some Quakers in Philadelphia had told him of the benefits to the United States that resulted from Hutchinson's death.

Note 57, Page 43.

" A gander has more brains by half:" and " A goose has got more sense by half;" are other readings of this line.

Note 58, Page 43.

Dr. Benjamin Rush: but the adjective does not agree with Mr. Adams's estimate, in 1775, of Rush's character. "He is an elegant, ingenious "body, a sprightly, pretty fellow. He is a republican. * * * But Rush, "I think, is too much of a talker to be a deep thinker; elegant, not "great."—*Life and Works*, II; 427. From circumstances, and his own talents, few men became more odious to the Tories than Rush: and he cordially reciprocated their sentiments. Smyth, who while in gaol at Philadelphia came into contact with him, styles him "a man eminent in "physic, but as eminent in rebellion, and still more so in unfulfilled pro- "fessions." But every thing that envy, hatred, malice, and all uncharitableness, ever did to vilify the character, conduct and connexions of Dr. Rush, pales beside the rancorous hatred and the powerful idiom of Cobbett, who actually kept up a periodical called *The Rush-Light*, with no other end or staple than witty abuse of the doctor and his friends: its motto was from *Job*:—"Can the rush grow up without mire? can the "flag grow without water? Whilst it is yet in his greenness, and not cut "down, it withereth before any other herb. So are the paths of all that "forget God; and the hypocrite's hope shall perish," &c. See *Porcupine's Works*, XII: *Index*.

Note 59, Page 43.

"Timothy Matlack, Esq., called from his cock-fighting propensities, "*Tim Gaff*."—*Duffield*.

Note 60, Page 43.

George Bryan, Esq.; born in Ireland, 1730; died in Pennsylvania, 27th January, 1791. He was prominent as a leader of the democratic wing of the Whig Party. See a previous Note: also *Reed's Reed*, II: *Index;* and *Littell's Graydon*, 287. "He was said to be a very diligent reader,
"and

" and was certainly a never weary monotonous talker, who, in the dif-
" courses he held, seldom failed to give evidence of the most minute, re-
" condite, and out of the way facts; insomuch, that a bet was once offered,
" that he could name the town-cryer of Bergen-op-Zoom."

NOTE 61, Page 44.

Alluding to the bribe alleged to have been tendered by Commodore Johnstone to General Reed; and refused: a matter that was the source of much comment on both sides of the Atlantic. The three persons involved; Johnstone, who offered the bribe; Mrs. Ferguson, who bore the message; and Reed, who repulsed it; had each a different version of the affair. Mrs. Ferguson admitting the truth of Reed's account, so far as he and Johnstone were concerned, at the same time denied that he had stated his conversation with her in either a fair, friendly, or kind manner. Johnstone declared there was not a word of truth in the whole story, and asserted that he had indisputable evidence in his possession to show that Reed's story was untrue. This evidence, he continued, could not be made public at the time, lest it should endanger the safety of private individuals; but he intimated that it should one day be given to the world. Its nature never has been made known: and there is little doubt but that the narratives of Reed and Mrs. Ferguson were substantially correct. Johnstone indeed admits that he used corrupt means in other instances; as truly there was reason to believe would have been attempted. Arthur Lee wrote from Paris to Congress in 1778, when Carlisle, Eden, and Johnstone were about setting forth as Royal Commissioners to America, that " the ministers of England give out that they have despatched half a
" million of guineas, to pave the way to a favourable reception of their pro-
" positions, and I know from the best authority here that they have assured
" Count Maurepas of their being *sure of a majority in Congress*." Lee was an enemy of Reed's,—(the same calumniator, wrote Franklin to Reed in 1780, " who formerly, in his private letters to particular mem-
" bers, accused you, with Messrs. Jay, Duane, Langdon, and Harrison,
" of

"of betraying the fecrets of Congrefs, in a correfpondence with the Minif-
"try:")—and his teftimony therefore as to the unworthy artifices to be employed, is of importance. A writer in Hall and Sellers' Gazette (Philadelphia, September 1ft, 1779), remarks with great earneftnefs on Johnftone's general avowal of the ufe of "other means befides perfuafion." He declares it to be the opinion "of many hardy zealots in our caufe," reafoning from the conduct of the Congrefs of 1778-9, that "it is impoffible that General
"Reed, whofe confequence in Congrefs was not of the firft order, could
"be the only member of that body who did not attract the notice of a
"bribe. To this great and good man a bribe was undeniably offered.
"It was no doubt offered to others. Gen. Reed was the only one who
"divulged, and therefore the only one who refufed it—for if offered to
"others, and that it muft have been offered to others befides the General,
"is next to a certainty, how came it to pafs (fay thefe fcrutinizing zealots)
"that they did not, like him, for reputation fake even, divulge the pro-
"ferred corruption?" If this infinuation had any real foundation, I cannot explain it: but if, as is moft likely, it was defigned to affect the political antagonifts of the local party to which Reed belonged, its explanation may confift in the facts already referred to in the Notes to *The Town Meeting*, of the hatred in which Robert Morris was then held by many; Mr. Morris, Mr. Dana, and Mr. Reed having each been addreffed, on his arrival, by letters from Johnftone. Governeur Morris and William Duer, Members of Congrefs from New York, were alfo, in 1779, on terms of political hoftility with General Reed.

Note 62, Page 44.

"*Vide the Letter from* Cleves *on the Lower Rhine*, in Dunlap's Penn-
"fylvania Packet, May 25th, 1779."—*Author's Note*. "Alluding to a
"piece publifhed in the faid paper founding the good Qualifications of
"Prefident Reed: *ftrongly fufpected to be compofed by himfelf.*"—*Manufcript Note*. This laft infinuation is probably falfe. The article in queftion was undoubtedly printed in Europe, and thence tranflated to America,

Mr.

Mr. C. G. F. Dumas, the Private Agent in Holland for American Affairs, wrote (4th November, 1778) from the Hague to the American Commissioners at Paris in this wise :—" The Courier of the Lower Rhine " contains a fine eulogy on Mr. Joseph Reed, member of Congress; it is " deserving of your attention. I wish I could send you the paper, but " I have only one copy, which I am about to forward to Congress." The following is the letter (probably altered to an English dress) as it appeared in Dunlap's Packet of May 25th, 1779.

Extract from a Gazette, printed at Cleves, on the Lower Rhine.

" The noble and disinterested conduct of the members of the American Congress, whom the British Commissioners endeavored to corrupt, has been received here with equal pleasure and admiration. They have generously disdained the most seducing offers that were made, and have therefore given the lie to the assertion of an Agent from the Court of London to that of Versailles, to a gentleman in high office.—' The end of this affair will prove that your nation has been the dupes of it. After you have made great efforts, and incurred immense expenses, to support American Independence, we shall purchase the Members of Congress, and the Congress itself: a little Gold distributed appropos will reëstablish us in all our rights, and cover you with shame for your proceedings.'—I am not worth purchasing, but such as I am, the King of Great Britain is not rich enough to do it! Virtuous and sublime Reed! Do not believe that we can pass over in silence a reply so magnanimous, so generous, worthy of being equalled to the finest expressions of patriotism and greatness of soul, of which the antient republics offer an example. Should this writing ever find its way to you, accept the homage which we pay to thy virtue, in the name of all those whose hearts know the worth of it. May your example find many imitators in your country, where baseness and venality have not made the fatal progress they have done in the countries of Europe! Such instances of magnanimity remind us that, four years ago, when the first steps towards independence were taken, we ventured to predict
' That

'That the Americans would exhibit examples of grandeur that would astonish our little souls.' And we have every day the satisfaction to see that we have not mistaken this extraordinary people, made to do honour to human nature, and to recall the idea of its primitive dignity."

Note 63, Page 45.

The fleet under D'Estaing was sent from France with a view to destroy the British squadron in the Delaware, and thus lend a vital assistance to the cause of America. Had it, instead, sailed directly to the West or East Indies or to other exposed possessions of England, it might doubtless have gained great advantages for France. The length of time D'Estaing was on the voyage, and the tidings that came to the English, enabled them to get on their guard; and the French on arrival found them gone to New York. After landing M. Gerard, the Minister, D'Estaing proceeded to Sandy Hook, where for eleven days, in the summer of 1778, he lay moored outside the bar. The pilots could not carry his largest ships over; and thus a smaller squadron, at New York under Howe, escaped the dubious conflict. The French admiral then went to Rhode Island, to coöperate with the American land forces under Sullivan against the British: where, after some skirmishing he was overtaken by a storm; and his fleet suffered much loss ere he could get into Boston. His flag-ship, the *Languedoc*, 90, lost her rudder and masts. The Americans were very angry at his leaving Newport and refusing to send any of his vessels back from Boston: and did not omit to publish their vexation in protests and general orders. While refitting at Boston (September, 1778), a serious row occurred between his people and some on the shore. Whether the last were Americans, or British prisoners, I do not know: but one or two of the French officers were dangerously, if not mortally wounded. A like occurrence was said to have occurred at Charleston, S. C., about the same period; when the French from their ships fired cannon and musketry, which the Americans retorted from the wharves. After his fleet was refitted, D'Estaing left Boston, for Martinique as was believed.

believed. The attempt at Newport, by the way, was a failure. The Americans were forced to retire when the French fleet no longer supported them.

Note 64, Page 45.

This is an early allusion to Tamenund, the Indian king, as the patron saint of America.

Note 65, Page 47.

Rev. George Duffield, a chaplain to Congress, and a Presbyterian. The allusion, that follows, to the attendance of Congress, at a Catholic Mass, refers to the willingness of that body, though Protestant, to pay a proper respect to the faith of the French King and of his Ambassador.

Note 66, Page 48.

We know that Odell was a French scholar; for in December, 1776, he acted as interpreter in that tongue between the Hessian commander and the people of Burlington, N. J.: but he does great injustice here to the prowess of the incomparable monarch of the Dipsodes, as described by Rabelais: who, after kicking the monstrous Loupgarou to death, seized his corpse by the two heels, and used it as a club to demolish the remainder of his enemies. " Finablement, voyant que tous estoyent mortz, " iecta le corps de Loupgarou tant qu'il peut contre la ville, et tumba " comme une grenouille sus le ventre en le place mage de ladicte ville, et " en tumbant du coup tua ung chat brusle, une chatte mouillee, une canne " petiere, et ung oyson bridé."—*La Vie de Gargantua et de Pantagruel:* liure ii. chap. xxix.

Note 67, Page 48.

Governor Samuel Huntington, of Connecticut, was President of Congress, in 1779 and 1780. M. de Chastellux was reminded by him of Fabricius, when he paid the President a visit and found his chamber lit by a solitary candle.

Note 68, Page 50.

Charles-Hector, comte D'Estaing, had served under Lally in India, and was captured at Madras by the English in 1759. He broke his parole: wherefore, being again taken prisoner, the English would not trust him, but lodged him in duresse. This circumstance gave birth to his continued animosity to Britain. His French biographer accuses him of time-serving in the civil turmoils of that kingdom: he testified against Marie Antoinette at her trial, and was presently guillotined in his own turn. M. de la Mothe Piquet was another French naval officer of distinction, who served on our coasts during the war.

Note 69, Page 50.

The Oneidas were the only tribe of the Six Nations in the interest of Congress. In 1779, Gen. Sullivan (whose objection to being left by D'Estaing at Newport, in 1778, as already referred to, gives point to this allusion) led an expedition against the hostile savages, and exchanged speeches with the Oneidas. Unless I am mistaken, Congress bestowed military rank upon several of the chiefs of this tribe: an inexpensive grant of honours, that probably suggested its repetition to the poet.

Note 70, Page 51.

The capture of the *Alcmene* frigate, October 21st, 1779, gave Rear Admiral Hyde Parker the first assurance of D'Estaing being gone to America.

Note 71, Page 52.

D'Estaing's first summons to Savannah was that it should surrender to the arms of the King of France. It may be noticed here, by the way, that the first news of the defence of Savannah reached New York on the
18th

18th November, 1779, five days only before that on which *The Feu de Joie* appeared in print. This evinces a rapidity of composition on the part of Dr. Odell. His story follows entirely the letters of Governor Tonyn and Colonel Fuser, which contained the intelligence referred to.

NOTE 72, Page 53.

Captain Moncrieffe was an old soldier, and a good one. His extensive acquaintance with this country, and the fact of his being the uncle of General Montgomery and the brother-in-law of Mr. Jay and Governor Livingston, had inspired a vain hope that he might adopt our cause. His services as Engineer Officer at Savannah were, in great part, the salvation of the place; and General Prevost, in his official report, declared that any mark of royal favour bestowed on Moncrieffe would be regarded as a personal gratification to every man in the army. He planned the works before Charleston in the following year, and received Clinton's most profuse praises in the Gazette. In a tract, published after the war, and written, it is suspected by Arnold, an anecdote is given of the battle of Brandywine. The English were advancing on the redoubt that Washington had thrown up to guard Chad's Ford, when Lieutenant Colonel (then Captain) Moncrieffe, who headed the column, saw an American howitzer, loaded with grape, pointed so as to rake the party, and the gunner about to apply the lighted match. "I'll put you to death if you fire!" Moncrieffe cried; on which the gunner dropped the match and fled. He died at New York, Dec. 10th, 1791; and was buried " in " Trinity Church, in the same tomb with his friend Colonel Maitland, " uncle to Lord Lauderdale, who, in dying, made it the last request that " his ashes should be mixed with my father's." See *Memoirs of Mrs. Margaret Coghlan*, Moncrieffe's daughter, and a very notorious woman, who numbered the Duke of York among her keepers.

Note 73, Page 53.

Colonel Maitland, an excellent officer, succeeded in getting into the town after the siege began. The relief he brought was very important, as the place, not expecting such an attack, was not strongly garrisoned. I have not seen this epitaph on him in print.

On the honourable Colonel Maitland, whose death was occasioned by the fatigues he suffered in his admired march from Beaufort to Savannah, and whose memory in the Charles Town Gazette receives its highest panegyrick from the mouth of an enemy. *By Mrs. De Lancey.*

> O'er *Maitland's* corpse as Victory reclin'd
> Reflecting on the fate of human kind:
> Is this, she cried, the end of all thy toils!
> What now avail thy laurels or thy spoils!
>
> Worn with fatigue thou cam'st thy friends to save—
> Saw them reliev'd, and sunk into the grave!
> Now grief and joy together blend their cries;
> Savannah's sav'd, yet generous Maitland dies.
> In vain around thy conq'ring soldiers weep:
> Thy eyes are clos'd in death's eternal sleep.
> Yet while a grateful King or Country sighs,
> O'er thy lov'd ashes marbles proud shall rise.
> Nay, even the Foe, reliev'd awhile from fear,
> Confess thy Virtues, and bestow a tear:
> Own, that as Valour strung thy nervous arm,
> So gentle Pity did thy bosom warm.
>
> O double praise—to make the haughty bend;
> Yet make the vanquish'd enemy a friend!
> Thus *Maitland* falls, though his undying name
> Shall live forever on the lips of Fame.

Note 74, Page 56.

Pulaſki had been one of the Confederates of Bar to ouſt Staniſlaus Poniatowſki from the Poliſh throne. Having ſkilfully ſeized and carried off the king, he and his party do not ſeem to have known what to do with him: they had not the means of long retaining him priſoner, and they were not willing to ſlay him; ſo Staniſlaus eſcaped, and Pulaſki fled the kingdom.

It is related, by one who was preſent, that in the moment of attack the advance on Savannah was delayed by the punctilio of an officer, whoſe company had failed to obtain the poſition of honour upon the right, to which military etiquette entitled it. Under a ſweeping fire of grapeſhot from the town, the whole diviſion was halted, while his company, with drum and fife, marched before the line to its place.

Note 75, Page 56.

This may refer to a ſmall ſortie on the night of Sept. 27th, which ſet the French and Americans firing on each other in the dark. Their loſs was ſaid to be about fifty. When the ſiege was about being given over, mutual civilities paſſed between the Engliſh and French officers, and one of the latter (Count O'Duin, an officer of rank) is reported by General Prevoſt as ſpeaking very acrimoniouſly of "the ſcoundrel Lincoln" and the Americans. General Benjamin Lincoln led our forces. Another Engliſh Officer mentioned a report that the Americans were offended at the ſummons to ſurrender to the French King only; and that the allies when they departed "were almoſt ready to cut one another's throats."

Note 76, Page 66.

Mariot Arbuthnot, nephew of Dr. John Arbuthnot the famous friend of Swift and Pope, was born in 1711, and died an Admiral of the Blue in 1794. In 1780, he commanded the naval forces at New York. When

When the French fleet came to Rhode-Island in July, 1780, Clinton wished to make a conjoined attack on the enemy there, but the Admiral, who was not only a bad tactician but a slow old man, did not act with sufficient haste, and all fell through. In recruiting at New York, he dropped a coarse remark which is not repeated in the text as here reprinted. Sir Henry Clinton in a Manuscript Note says: "It had been "proposed that 6000 men under Sir H. C. should have been landed in "Escourt Passage to meet the French on their embarkation: but as the "Admiral was not informed of their arrival till ten days after, and that "they had been reinforced and had had time to fortify, it would not "have been quite so prudent for the Army alone to attempt; and if the "Admiral had seen the propriety of taking an active part with the "Navy, he would have accepted the proposal of Sir H. C."

Note 77, Page 72.

The King's sloop *Savage*, of 16 guns, was lost near the river St. Lawrence before 1780: the *Triton* was a look-out vessel of Arbuthnot's fleet at New York in 1780.

Note 78, Page 72.

A place hard by New York where, it would appear, captive American Officers were often detained and boarded at two dollars a week. See *Littell's Graydon*: 245–255.

Note 79, Page 72.

Here is a confirmation of the assertion of the anonymous translator of Chastellux. Immense quantities of English, Spanish, and Portuguese gold coin were brought into America, during the war, at the cost of Great Britain: but "had all of them holes punched in them, or were otherwise "diminished at New York, before they were suffered to pass the lines; "from whence they obtained the name of *Robertsons* in the *rebel* country; "but

"but the profits, if any, of that commander, on this new edition of the coin, remain a secret." Major-General James Robertson was the last Royal Governor of New York: his jurisdiction never extended beyond the lines of the city.

Note 80, Page 74.

The manuscript of this Ode bears also the following obscure lines: "Dear Y—. Your scrap of Intelligence made a Mother's Eye glisten with delight and gratitude. Are not these feelings on these occasions finer than their lordly Masters. Your withering twig explains it in a moment. Well! I have executed all your commands, verbal and written, and now, feeling myself somewhat boulder after this full declaration, let me request the favor of you to put the above in a better dress than its own dad could invent or make for it: which will be doing as you would be done by. Benny will convince you I have not omitted sending a line, and that will evince this proposition that I am *wholly yours*. R. R. Tuesday morng."

Note 81, Page 79.

Fresh meats were so costly in New York during the war that the day commemorated by the poet was worthy of all his praise. Taking the prices for any year, we see how scarce fresh provisions must have been. In Feb. 1777, for instance, strong Irish butter was at 3s. per lb. In April, beef was at 14d. per lb.; butter at 2s.; mutton at 18d.; milk 7d. per quart; cabbages 20d. each, &c. In June, an egg was worth a shilling; in August, beef was at 21d. per lb., and other things in proportion. The Song also refers to the cherished idea with Washington and La Fayette of carrying New York. La Fayette was now in Virginia, acting against Arnold.

Note 82, Page 81.

The manuscript is addressed: "To Capt. Duncan. P. P.'s correc-"tion and alteration of the enclosed hasty dash is requested by the author." Captain Duncan was of the *Eagle*, Lord Howe's flagship, in 1778. The *Royal Oak*, 74, sailed from England with "the hardy Byron" in 1778, and was for several years in the American seas. M. Destouches was at Rhode-Island, in August, 1780, in command of *Le Neptune*, 74.

Note 83, Page 83.

Now *Burke*, with his *Prospect*, no longer can charm;
Nor Giants or Goblins the Nation alarm.—*Author's Variation*.

Note 84, Page 88.

To cast a slur on the character of Washington would, today, be the act, if of an American, of a very silly or a very dishonest man. The latitude of party heats and personal rivalries permitted a less restrained conduct during his life-time. The Tories had surely some excuse for speaking bitterly of the only man by whom the American Armies could have been led to Victory and Independence; for the vanquished party has in all times possessed at least the privilege of murmuring against its conqueror. But it must not be forgotten that long before and long after the War, as well as through its continuance, Washington was the object of the envy and the calumny of others than the adherents of the English crown. The earliest public outrage offered to his character appears in the official *Mémoire*, sent in 1756 by Louis XV to the other sovereigns of Europe, in which, referring to Washington's Ohio expedition and the death of Jumonville, in 1754, he says: "Il paroît que l'im-"posture ne coûte rien à M. Wasinghton; ici il s'en fait honneur." It is amusing to find that Beaumarchais in 1779, replying to Gibbon's state-ments and justifying the aid given by France to America, heads his list

of

of outrages exercised by England with this charge of assassination! He did not know that the falsehood hit the chief of the Americans, instead of the English court. Perhaps the original assertion by a foe of this bald slander " may be forgiven, though it cannot be applauded:" but its repetition was unfortunate on the lips of a friend. But the friends of America in the war were not all friends of Washington. His appearance in uniform in the Congress of 1775, and the military experience he had acquired, undoubtedly familiarized the minds of some members with the idea of his nomination to be Commander of the Army: but the consent of many of the delegates to this appointment was only extorted by the necessities of the case, and was a source "of real regret in nearly one half" of the gentlemen who made it. A number of the members were for Mr. Hancock; more were for Charles Lee; many for Washington; but the greatest number were in favour of Artemas Ward. There is room however for the inference that there was no desire on the part of a majority to maintain at the continental expense a New England army, with New England officers, to fight New England battles on New England soil. There was a Southern party against a Northern; "and so many of our
" stanchest men," says Adams, " were in the plan, that we could carry
" nothing without conceding to it. Another embarassment, which was
" never publicly known, and which was carefully concealed by those who
" knew it, the Massachusetts and other New England delegates were
" divided. Mr. Hancock and Mr. Cushing hung back; Mr. Paine did
" not come forward, and even Mr. Samuel Adams was irresolute. Mr.
" Hancock himself had an ambition to be appointed Commander-in-
" Chief * * * When I came to describe Washington for the commander,
" I never marked a more striking and sudden change of countenance.
" Mortification and resentment were expressed as forcibly as his (Han-
" cock's) face could exhibit them." Mr. C. F. Adams adds that " neither
" Hancock nor Ward was ever afterwards cordial towards" Washington. Nor were the Virginia delegates unanimous in his favour: " particularly
" Mr. Pendleton was very clear and full against it." When the question

was

was debated, there was a warm oppofition to Wafhington: on public, however, and not on any perfonal grounds. Pendleton, Sherman, Cufhing, and feveral others joined in it; fearing "difcontents in the army "and in New England." This army, it muft be recollected, confifted at that time almoft entirely of the men raifed by and in New England, and gathered before Bofton. There was in Congrefs a ftrong jealoufy of Maffachufetts, and a fufpicion of her real objects; and her reprefentatives were obliged to be very guarded in the expreffion of their fentiments, left other colonies fhould recoil from them. Wafhington's appointment, therefore, was juftly regarded by Adams as valuable, in fecuring the union of the colonies in defence of New England; and the troops forthwith raifed in the more fouthern provinces and fent thither by Congrefs juftified his predictions. And it muft likewife be remarked that at the time of the felection of Wafhington, Hancock writes favourably of the appointment. The pay of the General Officers was alfo a hard morfel for fome of the delegates to fwallow. Samuel and John Adams and Paine were earneft to reduce it, but in vain. "Thofe ideas of equality, which are fo agree-
"able to us natives of *New-England*, are very difagreeable to many gen-
"tlemen in the other Colonies. They had a great opinion of the high
"importance of a Continental General, and were determined to place
"him in an elevated point of light. They think the *Maffachufetts*
"eftablifhment too high for the privates, and too low for the officers, and
"they would have their own way." Probably the original fuggeftion of Wafhington for Commander-in-chief came from Johnfon of Maryland, or fome other Southern delegate; but to John Adams was due his public nomination. "Virginia is indebted to Maffachufetts for Wafhington," he boafted, "not Maffachufetts to Virginia. Maffachufetts made him a
"general againft the inclination of Virginia." But this can only refer to the voice of the delegates from thefe States, who were generally intimately allied in Congrefs on any party queftion. Long after the Peace, John Jay faid that in the Congrefs of the Revolution there was always, from firft to laft, a moft bitter party againft Wafhington. What were the

various

various motives of its members, it is impoffible to fay, fince their names even cannot, with fulnefs and accuracy, be now afcertained. It is but fair, however, to give the benefit of a doubt, and to fuppofe that it was an apprehenfion of the effect which fo much power and popularity might have on his ambition. The future was as yet unfeen; and many men knew not what would be the confequences of the attainment of Independence. "The fubjugation of my country," faid Edward Biddle, whofe declining health had compelled him to forego the influence his talents would have given him as delegate in Congrefs from Pennfylvania—" I "deprecate as a moft grievous calamity; and yet ficken at the idea of "thirteen, unconnected, petty democracies: if we are to be independ- "ent, let us, in the name of *God*, at once have an empire, and place "*Wafhington* at the head of it." But this idea was not pleafing to our people, whofe experience of the benefits of monarchy was not great, and very few of whom had ever been diftinguifhed by any royal favour; or, as an Englifh verfifier fang:

>Poor loft America, high honours miffing,
>Knows nought of fmile and nod, and fweet hand-kiffing:
>Knows nought of golden promifes of kings;
>Knows nought of coronets, and ftars, and ftrings:
>>In folitude the lovely rebel fighs!
>But vainly drops the penitential tear—
>>Deaf as the adder to the woman's cries,
>We fuffer not her wail to wound our ear:
>For food, we bid her hopelefs children prowl,
>And with the favage of the defert howl.

But fuch "fears of the brave and follies of the wife" are incident to human nature; and the jealoufy of Wafhington may have in fome cafes been connected with honeft though blind judgments. It was a public bleffing, thought Adams, that the glorious defence of the Delaware forts, in 1777, was "not immediately due to the Commander-in-chief nor to
"fouthern

"southern troops. If it had been, idolatry and adulation would have
"been unbounded; so excessive as to endanger our liberties, for what I
"know. Now, we can allow a certain citizen to be wise, virtuous and
"good without thinking him a deity or a Saviour." It was in the same
year that the writer took fire in Congress at the sentiments entertained for
the General by certain members: " I am distressed to find some of our
"members disposed to idolize an image which their own hands have
"molten. I speak of the superstitious veneration which is paid to General
"Washington. I honour him for his good qualities, but in this house,
"I feel myself his superior. In private life, I shall always acknowledge
"him to be mine." The *Cabal* against Washington was never more
violent than at this time, and probably debate ran high and warm language was used on either side: and his enemies, if we may rely on the
following anecdote, were more powerful in the Council-chamber than in
the Camp. In a *Life of Lord Stirling* the father-in-law of William Duer,
written by Mr. Duer's son (and the relationship is of some importance to
the authenticity of the anecdote), occurs this singular passage: " It is
"related by Mr. Dunlap in his History of New York, upon the authority
"it is presumed of the late General Morgan Lewis, that a day had been
"appointed by the *Cabal* in Congress for one of them to move for a
"Committee to proceed to the camp at Valley-Forge, to arrest General
"Washington; and that the motion would have succeeded had they not
"unexpectedly lost the majority which they possessed when the measure
"was determined on. At that time, there were but two delegates in
"attendance from New York; Francis Lewis, the father of the late
"General Morgan Lewis, and William Duer, the son-in-law of Lord
"Stirling—barely sufficient to entitle the State to a vote, if both were
"present. But Mr. Duer was confined to his bed by a severe and dan-
"gerous illness. His colleague, Mr. Lewis, had sent an express for Mr.
"Gouverneur Morris, one of the absent members, who however had not
"arrived on the morning of the day on which the motion was to have
"been made. Finding this to be the case, Mr. D. inquired of his phy-
"sician,

"fician, Dr. John Jones, whether it was poſſible for him to be carried
"to the Court-Houſe where Congreſs ſat. The Doctor told him it was
"poſſible, but it would be at the riſk of his life. 'Do you mean,' ſaid
"Mr. D., 'that I ſhould expire before reaching the place?' 'No,' re-
"plied the Doctor, 'but I would not anſwer for your leaving it alive.'
"'Very well, ſir,' ſaid Mr. D., 'you have done your duty, and I will
"do mine. Prepare a litter for me; if you will not, ſomebody elſe will—
"but I prefer your aid.' The litter was prepared, and the ſick man
"placed in it, when the arrival of Mr. Morris rendered the further uſe
"of it unneceſſary, and baffled the intrigue that had induced its prepara-
"tion." The date of this anecdote was ſuch as to render it extremely
improbable that the American Army, if it ſubmitted to Waſhington's
depoſal, would have ſtruck another blow under another leader for Congreſs. "I remember well," ſays a public writer in 1780, "that ſuch
"was the ſituation of the Army, while they lay at the Valley Forge in
"the winter of the year 1778, deſtitute of cloathing, many times in want
"of proviſions, and greatly diſcouraged, that a member of Congreſs, who
"had been on a Committee to the Camp to new model the troops with
"the advice of General Waſhington, declared to me, that 'ſuch had been
"the ſtate of things, that nothing but the great virtues of that man had
"kept the army together.'" Much concerning this *Cabal*, and its
workings in the Congreſs of 1778, exiſts in Gordon: whence it would
ſeem that delegates from Maſſachuſetts and Virginia were deep in the
affair. Samuel Adams, he ſays, was concerned in it, and adds: "The
"army was ſo confident of it, and ſo enraged, that perſons were ſtationed
"to watch him, as he approached the camp, on his return home. But
"he is commonly poſſeſſed of good intelligence, and was careful to keep
"at a ſafe diſtance. Had he fallen into the hands of the officers, when
"in that paroxiſm of reſentment, they would probably have handled him
"ſo as to have endangered his life, and tarniſhed their own honour."

There is a curious article in the *Pennſylvania Evening Poſt*, July 24th,
1779, which may refer to this anti-Waſhington Party in Congreſs: "a
"junto

" junto who have endeavored to subject all things to themselves, all power,
" civil military and marine: Who have endeavored to remove every
" person that would not mingle in their factious views; and to place none
" in office but their friends, relatives and dependents; against whose
" malevolence the unsullied fame of the great American patriot was but
" a slender barrier; whose victim was a W********— and whose idol
" was a L**." The same journal (July 9th, 1779) mentions the existence in Congress of a sort of Club of certain New England, New Jersey, and Pennsylvania delegates, with two or three from the Southward; the foundation of which had been laid in the first Congress, when there was cause to fear that New York and one or two other Middle Colonies were averse to extreme measures. Among the Washington party in Congress, I should put such names as those of Robert, Lewis, and Gouverneur Morris; Jay; Paca; Burke; Drayton; Duane; Duer; Francis Lewis. The question is not so clear in regard to Samuel Adams; Mifflin; Witherspoon; Rush; Jefferson; the Lees, &c.; though any conclusion to be arrived at must in some measure be conjectural. In 1789, Samuel Adams in a manner denied to a friend the truth of Dr. Gordon's statement of his having been concerned in a plot to remove Washington. And in 1796, when John Adams was a successful candidate for the Presidency of the United States, he makes an observation that would imply a well-established community of action between Samuel Adams and Thomas McKean:
" The feelings of friendship excite a curiosity to know how McKean will
" vote. By that I shall guess how Governor Adams would have voted."
On April 4th, 1778, Patrick Henry wrote to Richard Henry Lee that he (Lee) was traduced in Virginia by persons who alleged that he was engaged in a scheme to discard Washington: and in 1780, Dr. William Shippen, jun. wrote thus to him of General Greene: " He is a little
" suspicious that you are not perfectly satisfied with his conduct, because
" you were said to be inimical to our commander, and of consequence
" to him, who was supposed to be one of his flatterers—this false
" idea I have reprobated to General Greene, and assured him he would
                                                                    " find

"find you his friend and useful confidant." And it is said also that the occasion of Lee's losing his popularity at home, and his seat in Congress in 1777, was chiefly because he had compelled his tenants to pay their rents. His biographer and namesake, in several places, flouts the charge made by Judge Johnson, in the *Life of Greene*, that Richard Henry Lee was Washington's enemy. But if Samuel Adams was, so was, probably, Lee. It is at all events a gratifying thing to remark that no one, in later days, had the moral courage to confess that he was concerned in the business; indeed its very name of *Conway's Cabal* shows that its members were afraid or ashamed to avow their complicity; for Conway was but a tool of the hour, whom it was easy enough for a fellow-soldier to silence, and whose name was affixed to a scheme (that he doubtless approved of, but which was concocted by longer heads than his own) merely to avert the attention of the world from its real authors. In the Army, indeed, the love and veneration for Washington was boundless, and almost universal; and here truly lay the stumbling-block of his enemies. It was only in the immediate circle of some of the foreign-born officers, as Conway, Lee, and Gates, that an opposite opinion was heard. Lee's sentiments in regard to "Washington and his puppies" are sufficiently well known. "*Entre nous*" he says to Gates in December, 1776, "a certain great man is "damnably deficient." "As to his talents for the command of an army," said Gates to Graydon, 'with a French shrug,' "they were miserable "indeed." The testimony of the civilian, who was forced to remove from a comfortable house in one place to a comfortable house in another, because Washington, with vastly inferior forces could not drive Howe out of Philadelphia, would be amusing but for the circumstance that, himself in a position to obtain a comfortable dinner—" a good roast turkey, plain "pudding, and minced pies"—he could so grievously have misconceived the condition of the Army in his vicinity. As Mr. William B. Reed justly observes, "the sufferings of the Americans during their winter canton- "ment at the Valley Forge have been often described. They have never "been exaggerated." Yet in the end of December, 1777, after noticing

Howe's

Howe's movements, a Pennfylvania Whig remarks: "All this is done in the view of our Generals and our army, who are carelefs of us, but carefully confulting where they fhall go to fpend the winter in jollity, gaming and caroufing. O tell not this in France or Spain! Publifh it not in the ftreets of London, Liverpool or Briftol, left the uncircumfifed there fhould rejoice, and fhouting for joy, fay "America is ours, for the rebels are difmayed and afraid to fight us any longer! O Americans, where is now your virtue?. O Wafhington, where is your courage?" In this Note, no citation is made of Tory or Britifh accufations againft Wafhington. One of thefe was, however, againft his chaftity: and fome of the charges went fo far as to identify the woman and to trace the offfpring. This is only recurred to here, becaufe of a like infinuation being made apparently by Charles Lee, to General Reed, in 1778; but with great propriety the latter repelled as unworthy of credence the flanders that charged the Commander-in-chief with "great cruelty to his flaves in Virginia, and immorality of life, though they acknowledge it is fo very fecret that it is difficult to detect it."

In the clofe of 1779, General Sullivan warned Wafhington that the *Cabal* of 1777 againft him ftill exifted, and waited only for fufficient ftrength to attack him openly. He therefore advifes him to keep on his guard. "Appearances may deceive even an angel. Could you have believed, four years ago, that thofe adulators, thofe perfons fo tenderly and fo friendly ufed, as were Gates, Mifflin, Reed, and Tudor, would become your fecret and bitter, though unprovoked enemies. If we view them now, we cannot help lamenting the want of fincerity in mankind."

But everything faid or done during the War, by Whig or Tory, falls far fhort of the dreadful charges brought againft Wafhington by his political opponents and fellow-citizens in 1795, 1796, and 1797. Compared with the language of *Valerius, Pittachus, A Calm Obferver, &c.*, former fcurrility almoft became praife. Every variety of evil, from avarice and fraud to tyranny and murder, was imputed to his hands, with a power of conception and expreffion that leaves us no room to wonder

wonder that he should have disdained to run the gauntlet of a third presidential term; that " he prudently retreated," to quote the remark of his successor. "Will not the world be led to conclude," says one, "that the " mask of political hypocrisy has been alike worn by a Cæsar, a Crom- " well and a Washington!" " Had the meridian blaze of the President's " popularity continued much longer," writes another, " the lamp of " American liberty would have been extinguished forever. Happily for " humanity, a change has taken place before it was too late, and the con- " secrated ermine of presidential Chastity seems too foul for time itself to " bleach." In the *Philadelphia Aurora*, a paper edited with detestable ability, will be found scores of pieces of a like nature. What can be more lamentable than such lines as these, published at the very epoch (March 4th, 1797) of Washington's withdrawal to private life? " 'Lord, " lettest now thy servant depart in peace, for mine eyes have seen thy " salvation,' was the pious ejaculation of a man who beheld a flood of " happiness rushing in upon mankind. If ever there was a time, that " would license the reiteration of the exclamation, that time is now " arrived: for the man who is the source of all the misfortunes of our " country, is this day reduced to a level with his fellow-citizens, and is " no longer possessed of a power to multiply evil upon the United States. " If ever there was a period for rejoicing, this is the moment. Every " heart in unison with the freedom and happiness of the people, ought to " beat high with exultation that the name of Washington from this day " ceases to give a currency to political iniquity, and to legalize corrup- " tion—a new æra is now opening upon us, an æra which promises much " to the people; for public measures must now stand upon their own " merits, and nefarious projects can no longer be supported by a name. " When a retrospect is taken of the Washingtonian administration for eight " years, it is a subject of the greatest astonishment, that a single individual " should have cankered the principles of republicanism in an enlightened " people, just emerged from the gulf of despotism, and should have carried " his designs against public liberty so far, as to have put in jeopardy its

" very

"very exiftence: fuch, however, are the facts, and with thefe ftaring us "in the face, this day ought to be a *jubilee* in the United States." In 1813, John Adams, writing to Jefferfon, refers to "the terrorifm excited "by Genet, in 1793, when 10,000 people in the ftreets of Philadelphia, "day after day, threatened to drag Wafhington out of his houfe, and "effect a revolution in the government, or compel it to declare war in "favor of the French revolution and againft England. The cooleft and "the firmeft minds, even among the Quakers in Philadelphia, have given "their opinions to me, that nothing but the yellow fever, which removed "Dr. Hutchinfon and Jonathan Dickinfon Sergeant from this world, "could have faved the United States from a fatal revolution of govern- "ment." But Adams's morbid jealoufy of every one whofe fame out- fhone or even (in his own opinion) rivalled his own, cankers very many of his judgments on Wafhington. While Prefident himfelf, he complained that he was annoyed by "puppets, danced upon the wires of two jugglers "behind the fcenes; and thefe jugglers were Hamilton and Wafhington." In another and (as believed) unpublifhed manufcript, he fays (Aug. 23rd, 1806): "The Federalifts, as they are called by themfelves and their "enemies, have done themfelves and their country incalculable injury by "making Wafhington their political, religious, and even moral pope, and "afcribing every thing to him. Hancock, Samuel Adams, ———, and "feveral others have been much more effential characters to America, than "Wafhington. Another character, almoft forgotten, of more importance "than any of them all, was James Otis. It is to offend againft Eternal "juftice to give to one, as this people do, the merits of fo many. It is "an effectual extinguifher of all patriotifm and all public virtue, and "throws the nation entirely into the hands of intrigue. You lament the "growth of corruption very juftly; but there is none more poifonous "than the eternal puffing and trumpetting of Wafhington and Franklin, "and the inceffant abufe of the real Fathers of the country."

Defpite all that has been faid too of Mr. Jefferfon's relations with Wafhington, it is difficult to hold that thefe really could have been of a

perfectly

perfectly sincere and friendly nature. It was believed in Washington's family that shortly before his death he opened his mind very plainly to Mr. Jefferson, in two or three letters. A gentleman, who was Washington's confidential clerk at the time, gives us some idea of their nature; for neither letters nor copies long continued in existence after their writer was dead. "The first was," he said, "rather a letter of inquiry; the second one "was so severe, and excited his feelings so much, that the hair appeared "to rise on his head as he recorded it, and he felt that it must produce a "duel—that the third was of a milder tone, but not a very gratifying "one."

It is not, at this day, too much to say, that the common suffrage of all that is wise and good in human nature, authorizes us to question that man's soundness of judgment or rectitude of purpose, who impugns the character of *George Washington*.

INDEX.

ABERCROMBIE, Rev. James, 6.
Achilles, xi.
Adams, Charles F., 177.
 John, 102, 113, 121, 122, 123, 124, 136, 139, 143, 149, 159, 162, 163, 164, 177, 178, 179, 180, 185, 186.
  on the Howes, 139.
  on the Pennsylvania Constitution, 121.
  on the Quakers, 123, 124.
  on Dr. W. Smith, 143.
  nominates Washington, 177, 178.
  sentiments towards Washington, 185, 186.
 Samuel, 113, 149, 162, 177, 178, 181, 182, 186.
  said to oppose Washington, 177, 181, 182.
  denies it, 182.
  threatened by army, 181.
Agincourt, 2.
Alcides, 24, 25.
Alcmene (frigate), 170.
Alexandria, 162.
Amboy, 137.
Americanisms, 36, 39, 157.
André, Major John, 115.
Andromeda, 54.
Annapolis, 160.
Anson, Lord, 62.

Arbuthnot, Dr. John, 173.
 Adm. Mariot, 66, 82, 136, 173, 174.
 notice of, 173.
Armitage, B., 117.
Arnold, Benedict, 40, 79, 118, 156, 159, 171, 175.
 book attributed to, 171.
Assembly balls, 160.
Astræa, 24.
Aurora, denounces Washington, 185.

BAILEY, Francis, 99.
Bank of Pennsylvania, 157.
Banks, Sir Joseph, 113.
Bar, confederates of, 173.
Bayard, James A., 156.
 John, 39, 43, 156.
Baylor's dragoons, 154.
Beaufort, Cardinal, xiii.
Beaumarchais, 176.
Beck, Paul, 155.
Bellona, 9, 63.
Benezet, Mr., 155.
Biddle, Edward, wishes Washington for king, 179.
Bingham, William, 158.
Blake, Adm. Robert, 62.
Brag, ———, 158.
Brandywine, 134, 138, 171.
 anecdote of, 171.
Bradford, Wm., 152.
Bray, John, 162.
 Vicar of, 86.

Index.

British success in 1759, 18, 130.
Browne, Sir Thomas, xi.
Brunswick, 137.
Bryan, George, 43, 118, 122.
    notice of, 164.
Bull, John, 139.
    Col. John, 42, 162.
Bunker-hill, 134.
Bunyan, John, xiv.
Burd, Mr., 155.
Burgoyne, Sir John, 25, 36, 68, 138, 147.
Burgoyne's defeat, 160.
Burke, Edmund, 83, 176.
    (of America), 182.
Burleigh, Lord, 4.
Burlington, 7, 9, 39, 169.
Burne, the barber, 159.
Byron, Admiral John, 176.

CABAL against Washington, 180, 182.
Cadwalader, Gen. John, 122.
Camillo Querno, 105.
Cæsar, 2, 141, 185.
Campaign, the success of the, 160.
Campbell, George, 155.
    Captain, 155.
Canada, 130, 140.
Cannon, James, 122.
Carlisle, Earl of, 165.
Carleton, Sir Guy, 84, 140, 141.
Carpenter's Hall, 61, 155.
Cary, Mr., 113.
Cato, 34.
Chalmers, George, 136.
Chambers, Colonel, 155.
Chambly, 7.
Charles First, x.
    Second, 29, 30, 81.
Charlotte, Queen, 14, 116.
Chastellux, M. de, 160, 169, 174.

Chew, Benjamin, 125, 138.
Chubb, R., 14.
Church-and-King club, 147.
Cleves, letter from, 166.
Clinton, Sir Henry, 63, 66, 67, 77, 79, 82, 114, 138, 141, 171, 174.
    private comments on Howe, 138; on Arbuthnot, 174.
Clinton's Retreat, 160.
Clymer, Daniel, 155.
    George, 155.
Cobbett, William, 101, 121, 164.
Cocytus, 73.
Coffin, Mr. 17, 18, 129, 139.
Coghlan, Mrs. Margaret, 171.
Coldspring, 9.
Collins, Mrs., 98.
Congress, 36, 143, 144, 165, 169, 180.
Constitution of Pennsylvania, 122, 124, 158.
Conway, Marshal, 144.
    Gen. Thomas, 183.
Cooper, Rev. Dr. Myles, 105.
    William, 133.
Cornwallis, Lord, 138.
Craft, James, 115.
Cressy, 2.
Cromwell, Oliver, x, 134, 185.
Cushing, Thomas, 177, 178.

DANA, Francis, 166.
Dastouche, Adm., 82.
De Berdt, Denis, 134, 137.
De Graffe, Count, 157.
De Lancey, Mrs., lines by, 172.
Delaney, Sharpe, 155.
Delight (ship), 157.
D'Estaing, M., 45, 50, 51, 53, 56, 168, 170.
D'Estouches, M., 82, 176.

De Ruyter, Capt., 145.
Dickinson, John, 152.
Dipsodes, the, 169.
Drake, Sir Francis, 62.
Drayton, William, 182.
Dryden, xvi.
Duane, James, 143, 165, 182.
Duer, William, 166, 180, 182.
Duffield, Edward, 148, 160, 164.
    Rev. George, 47, 169.
Dumas, C. G. F., 167.
Duncan, Captain, 176.
Dunlap, William, 180.

EAGLE (ship). 176.
    Eden, William, 165.
Edinburgh, 139.
Elizabeth, Queen, 4.
Eloisa, 109.
Emlen, Samuel, 162.
Experiment, the, 35, 146.
    captured, 145.

FABRICIUS, 169.
    Fallon, Dr., 160.
Ferguson, Mrs. Elizabeth, 165.
First City Troop, 126, 154.
Fisher, Joshua Francis, xvi.
Flatbush, 72, 174.
Fletcher, Andrew, xii.
Fooks, Paul, 117.
Fothergill, Dr., 145.
Franklin, Benjamin, 5, 45, 112, 113, 122, 134, 136, 165, 186.
    Arthur Lee's opinion of him, 113.
    John Adams on, 186.
    Howe's hopes from, 134, 136.
Franklin's Stove, authorship of its inscription, 112.

Fuser, colonel L. V., 171.

GALLOWAY, Joseph, 141.
    Gargantua, 169.
Gates, Gen. Horatio, 15, 118, 120, 147, 157, 183, 184.
    dislikes Washington, 183, 184.
Genet, M., 186.
George III, 7, 9, 13, 75, 77, 80, 83, 89, 113, 140.
Gérard, M., 168.
Germain, Lord George, 138, 141.
Germantown, 41, 138, 154, 159.
Gerry, Elbridge, 162.
Geyer, Caspar, 104.
Ghent, 156.
Gibbon, Edward, 176.
Gordon, Rev, William, 181, 182.
Goshen, 42, 163.
Grant, General, 138.
Grasse, M. de, 157.
Graydon, Alexander, 122, 183.
Grayson, Colonel, 155.
Greene, Gen. Nath., 137, 182.

HAMILTON, Alexander, 133, 186.
    William, 83.
Hamlet, xiv.
Hancock, John, 126, 177, 178, 186.
    aspires to command the army, 177.
    thought by Adams of more account than Washington, 186.
Hannibal, 84.
Hardie, captain, 41, 160.
Hardinge, George, 116.
Harrison, Benjamin, 165.
Hawke, Adm. Edward, 62.
Hazen's regiment, 155.

Henry, Patrick, 182.
Hermes, 24, 25, 142.
Hessians, 47, 56, 138.
High-street Ward, 156.
Hillegas, Michael, 41, 157, 160.
Hillsborough, Lord, 113.
Hopkinson, Francis, 23, 69.
Howe, George viscount, 140.
    Richard, earl, 36, 128, 134, 135, 136, 137, 139, 140, 142, 168, 176.
    consults Franklin, 134, 136.
    expects to make peace, 134, 135, 136.
    his flagship, 176.
    Sir William, 10, 13, 17, 19, 23, 36, 98, 115, 117, 118, 123, 128, 129, 130, 131, 134, 137, 138, 139, 140, 141, 142, 144, 183.
    suspected of being secretly concerned in trade, 129, 139, 140.
    his proclamation, 19, 131.
    Clinton's criticisms on him, 138.
    notice of, 134-142.
    his amours, 23, 25, 141.
Humphreys, Daniel, 119.
    James, 13.
Huntingdon, Countess of, 113, 114, 115.
Huntington, Samuel, 48, 169.
Hutchinson, Dr. James, 45, 163, 186.

INDEPENDENCE, Declaration of, 14, 116, 136, 137, 153, 179.
Inglis, Captain, 157.
Ingraham, Edward D., 148.
Irish beef, 21, 132.

JAY, John, 165, 171, 178, 182.
    charged with treachery, 165.
Jay's Treaty, 158.
Jefferson, Thomas, 182, 186, 187.
    roughly handled by Washington, 187.
Jesuit's bark, cargo captured, 145.
Job, 164.
Johnson, Thomas, 178.
Johnstone, Com. George, 44, 165, 166.
Jones, Dr. John, 181.
Jove, 23.
Judas, 57.
Jumonville, M. de, 176.
Juno, 24.

KILLIGREW, Thomas, 29.
Kinsey, James, 134.

LA Belle Poule captured, 146.
Lafayette, M. de, 67, 79, 175.
Lally, Count, 170.
Langdon, John, 165.
Languedoc, 168.
Lanyard, Jack, 61.
Lauderdale, Lord, 171.
Lawrence, Thomas, 155.
Lee, Arthur, 113, 165.
    Gen. Charles, 141, 142, 177, 182, 183, 184.
    his opinion of Washington, 142, 184.
    Mrs. Charles, xvi.
    Richard Henry, his enmity to Washington asserted and denied, 182, 183.
    Fort, 137.
Legal Paper Money, 17, 29, 128, 130, 131, 143.

Legere frigate deftroyed, 146.
Lenox, Major David, 154.
Lewis, Francis, 180, 182.
    Gen. Morgan, 180.
Lincoln, Gen. Benjamin, 51, 52, 57, 173.
Livingfton, William, 133, 143, 171.
Long Ifland, 134, 137.
Loring, Mrs., 23.
Loughborough, Lord, 139.
Louis XV, 176.
    XVI, 45, 52.
Loupgarou, 169.
Lucifer, 6.

MACARONI privateer, 157.
    McClenachan, Blair, 40, 153, 157, 158.
McKean, Thomas, 41, 157, 161, 182.
M'Lane, Allan, 155.
Maitland, Colonel, 51, 53, 171, 172.
Mann, Sir Horace, 139.
Marie Antoinette, 170.
Mars, 24.
Marfhall, Chriftopher, 133, 184.
Mafon, the double, 40.
Matlack, Timothy, 42, 43, 161, 164.
Maurepas, Count, 165.
Meafe, James, 15, 120.
Mifflin, John T., 155.
    Gen. Thomas, 154, 182, 184.
Minden, 2.
Mitchell, Col. John, 41, 157, 160, 161.
Moncrieffe, Major, 51, 53, 171.
Montgomery, Gen. Richard, 7, 29, 144, 171.
Morgan, Colonel, 126.
Morris, Charles M., xvi.

Morris, Gouverneur, 166, 180, 181, 182.
    Lewis, 182.
    Robert, 40, 121, 122, 131, 151, 152, 153, 155, 157, 159, 162, 166, 182.
    Samuel C., 155.
Mothe, M. Piquet de la, 50, 170.
Mufgrave, Colonel, 138.

NAPOLEON, 134.
    Neptune, 62.
    Le, 176.
New England, 137.
Newton, Sir Ifaac, 5.
New York, 132, 138, 175.
Niagara, 130.
Nichols, General, 155.
Nixon, John, 117.
Norris, Mifs Deborah, 112.
North, Lord, 140, 141.
Nottingham, 142.

ODELL, Dr. Jonathan, verfes by, 5, 7, 9, 11, 45, 51, 58, 105, 106, 108, 110, 111.
    notices of, xv, xvii, 105, 106, 112, 113, 169, 171.
    Mifs Molly, 110.
O'Duin, Count, 173.
Oneidas, 50, 170.
Otis, James, 186.
Ovid, 162.

PACA, William, 182.
Paine, Robert Treat, 177.
Paine, Thomas, 137.
Pantagruel, 48, 169.
Paper money, 41, 149, 150, 153, 161.
Paris, 131.

Parker, Adm. Sir Hyde, 47, 51, 170.
Paschall, Benjamin, 40, 159.
Patterson, Mr., 157.
Pemberton, James, 162.
    John, 162.
Pendleton, Edmund, 177, 178,
Penington, Edward, 125, 127.
    Isaac, 125.
Penn, William, 125.
Pennyfeather, land of, 26.
Pennsylvania, bank of, 157.
    Constitution of 1776, 122, 124, 149, 158.
    its formation, 122.
    obnoxious to many, 122.
Pepys, Samuel, 121.
Perseus, 54.
Peters, Richard, 15, 119, 120.
Philadelphia, 95, 129, 130, 131, 132, 138, 143, 144, 150, 153, 156, 159, 162, 163, 185, 186.
    Aurora attacks Washington, 185.
Piercy, Rev. William, 6, 113.
    notice of, 113.
Pilkington, Rev. M., 34.
Pindar, Peter, xvii, 113, 179.
Plato, 34.
Plymouth, 136.
Poictiers, 2.
Poniatowski, king Stanislaus, 175.
Pope, Alexander, 108, 173.
    Edith, 108.
Potts, John, 155.
Prevost, Gen. Aug., 51, 53, 54, 171, 173.
Price, Mr., 17, 18.
Princeton, 138.
Proclamation, 131.
Pulaski, Count Casimir, 55, 173.

QUAKERS, 14, 17, 117, 122, 123, 127, 130, 144, 163, 186.
Quebec, 2, 130.
Querno, Camillo, 105.

RABELAIS, Francis, 169.
Rattlesnake, the, 159.
Reed, Gen. Joseph, 44, 69, 134, 152, 154, 156, 157, 165, 166, 167, 184.
    is variously accused, 44, 156, 165, 166, 184.
    William B., 183.
Regiment, Lines on 23rd, 106.
Reynolds, John, 162.
Rivington, James, 39, 45, 63, 99, 157.
Roberdeau, Gen. Daniel, 6, 42, 151, 156, 162, 163.
Robertson, Lieut. Gen. James, 175.
Robertsons, or clipt coins, 174.
Robinson, Andrew, 155.
Rodney, Adm. Lord, 77, 83, 157.
Royal Oak, the, 81, 176.
Rush, Dr. Benjamin, 43, 157, 164, 182.
Rushlight, the, 164.
Russel, Admiral, 62.

SANDY Hook, 48, 137, 168.
Savage, the, 72, 174.
Savannah, 51, 53, 170, 172, 173.
Schaffer, John, 155.
Scott, Sir Walter, 141.
Sergeant, Jonathan D., 186.
Shelah, the, 72.
Sherman, Roger, 178.
Shippen, Dr. Wm., 182.
Simcoe, Col. John G., 141.
Smith, Robert, 104.
    William, 104.

Index. 195

Smith, Rev. William, 29, 112, 143.
    Mr., 33, 103.
Smyth, J. F. D., 164.
Sodom, 43.
Sproat, Mr., 113.
St. Andrew, 45.
St. Clair, Gen. Arthur, 122.
St. David, 45.
St. Dennis, 45.
St. George, 1, 4, 45, 74, 76, 102.
St. John's, 7, 115.
St. Patrick, 45.
St. Paul's Churchyard, 98.
St. Tammany, 45, 169.
Stansbury, David, 102.
    Joseph, verses by, 1, 3, 4, 6, 10, 13, 14, 16, 17, 19, 20, 22, 23, 25, 29, 31, 33, 34, 36, 37, 38, 39, 61, 63, 64, 66, 68, 69, 81, 83, 84, 86, 88, 89, 90, 95, 100.
    notice of, xv., 95-102, 129, 130, 131, 142, 143, 156.
    Mrs., 90, 97.
Staten Island, 137.
Stewart, Charles, 136.
Stirling, Gen. Lord, 180.
Sturdy Beggar, the, 159.
Success of the Campaign, 160.
Sullivan, Gen. John, 123, 142, 168, 170, 184.
Swift, Dr. Jonathan, 173.

TAMENUND, 45, 169.
    Tarleton, Col. Banastre, xii,
Thompson, Gen. Wm., 155.
Ticonderoga, 130.
Titan, 41.
Tonyn, Gov. Patrick, 171.
Tories, 133, 153, 163, 164, 176.
Town Meeting, the, 148.
Towne, Benjamin, 20.

Trenton, 39, 138.
Trinity Church, 171.
Triton, 72, 174.
Troop, First City, 154.
Tudor, William, 184.
Twenty-third regiment, welcome to, 106.
Twickenham, 108,.
United States, 89.
    debt, 149.
Uther, ix.

VALLEY-FORGE, 180, 183.
    Venus, 23, 24, 25.
Ville de Paris, 157, 158.
Virgil, 162.

WALLACE, Sir James, 35, 145.
Walpole, Horace, 139.
Ward, Gen. Artemas, 177.
Warren, James, 136.
Warwick, earl of, xvi.
Washington, 46, 79, 84, 88, 120, 125, 133, 136, 138, 139, 142, 158, 175, 176-187.
    obstacles to his appointment, 177, 178.
    distrusted in congress, 177, 179, 180, 181, 182, 183, 184.
    confided in by army, 181, 183.
    desired as Emperor, 179.
    plan for his arrest, 180.
    charged with various offences, 88, 176, 177, 184.
    John Adams on, 136, 186.
    Beaumarchais on, 176.
    Gates on, 183.
    Charles Lee on, 142, 183, 184.
    Louis XV on, 176.
    Philadelphia Aurora on, 185

Washington, his plans against New York, 46, 79, 175.
   reviled by newspapers, 184.
   threatened with violence, 186.
   deterred from further public life, 185.
   his retirement welcomed by some, 185.
   persons said to be hostile to him, 182, 184, 187.
   strong letters to Jefferson, 187.
Washington, fort, 137.
Watson, Elkanah, 114.
   John F., 154, 156, 160.
Watson's Annals, 148.
Wedderburne, Alexander, 139.
Wellington, 140.
Wells, R., 30, 101.
Wharton, Fishbourne, 126.
   Thomas, 125.
Whitefield, Rev. George, 114.
Whitemarsh, 23.
Will, William, 41, 160.
Wilkinson, Col. James, 161.
Willing, Richard, 15, 121.
   Thomas, 15, 121, 142, 143.
Wilson, James, 143, 153, 155, 156.
   threatened with violence, 153.
Wistar, William, 40, 159.
Witherspoon, Rev. John, 182.
Wolcot, John, xvii, 113, 116, 179.
Waxall, Sir Nathaniel, 140.
Wright, Abijah, 104.

YEATES, Judge Jasper, 112.
   York, duke of, 171.

LIST OF SUBSCRIBERS.

LARGE PAPER COPIES.

1	J. Carson Brevoort;	Brooklyn.
2	John Carter Brown;	Providence.
3	James Lenox;	New York.
4	William Menzies;	New York.
5	Winthrop Sargent;	Natchez.

SMALL PAPER.

1	S. Alofsen;	Jerfey City.
2	American Antiquarian Society;	Worcefter.
3	Astor Library;	New York.
4	N. P. Bailey;	Kingfbridge, N. Y.
5	George Bancroft;	New York.
6	Samuel L. M. Barlow;	New York.
7	J. R. Bartlett;	Providence.
8	J. Carson Brevoort;	New York.
9	Charles I. Bushnell;	New York.
10	William Allen Butler;	New York.
11	Erastus Corning;	Albany.
12	William J. Davis;	New York.
13	Gilbert C. Davidson;	Albany.
14	Henry B. Dawson;	Morrifania.
15	Smith Ely, Jr.;	New York.

16	JOHN FOWLER, JR. ;	New York.
17	ELI FRENCH (3 copies) ;	New York.
20	BENJAMIN H. HALL ;	Troy.
21	WILLIAM HOWARD HART ;	Troy.
22	Z. HOSMER ;	Boston.
23	ALLAN McLEAN HOWARD ;	Toronto.
24	WALDO HUTCHINS ;	New York.
25	JAMES B. KIRKER ;	New York.
26	GEORGE LAW ;	New York.
27	LIBRARY COMPANY ;	Philadelphia.
28	BENSON J. LOSSING ;	Poughkeepsie.
29	HENRY S. McCALL ;	Albany.
30	MAINE HISTORICAL SOCIETY ;	Brunswick.
31	WILLIAM G. MEDLICOTT ;	Longmeadow, Mass.
32	WILLIAM MENZIES ;	New York.
33	MERCANTILE LIBRARY ASSOCIATION ;	New York.
34	MERCANTILE LIBRARY SOCIETY ;	Baltimore.
35	MILITARY ACADEMY ;	West Point.
36	CHARLES C. MOREAU ;	New York.
37	JOHN B. MOREAU ;	New York.
38	T. BAILEY MYERS ;	Mosholu, N. Y.
39	NEW YORK STATE LIBRARY ;	Albany.
40	HENRY NICOLL ;	New York.
41	CHARLES B. NORTON (5 copies) ;	New York.
46	OHIO STATE LIBRARY ;	Columbus.
47	RICHARD H. PHELPS ;	Windsor, Ct.
48	G. W. PRATT ;	New York.
49	J. V. L. PRUYN ;	Albany.
50	JOEL RATHBONE ;	Albany.
51	C. B. RICHARDSON ;	New York.
52	GEORGE W. RIGGS, JR. ;	Washington.
53	JOHN A. RUSSELL ;	New York.
54	WINTHROP SARGENT (5 copies) ;	Natchez.

64	David Sears;	Boston.
65	J. Gilmary Shea;	New York.
66	Henry A. Smith;	Cleveland.
67	W. B. Sprague, Jr.;	Albany.
68	J. Austin Stevens;	New York.
69	Robert Townsend;	Albany.
70	Howard Townsend;	Albany.
71	Franklin Townsend;	Albany.
72	Frederick Townsend;	Albany.
73	W. B. Trask;	Boston.
74	Wm. H. Tuthill;	Tipton, Iowa.
75	Townsend Ward (10 copies);	Philadelphia.
85	Wm. H. Whiteman;	Philadelphia.
86	W. H. Whitmore;	Boston.
87	H. Austin Whitney;	Boston.
88	Wm. A. Young;	Albany.

www.ingramcontent.com/pod-product-compliance
Lightning Source LLC
Chambersburg PA
CBHW031826230426
43669CB00009B/1243